praise for *follow me*

"*Follow Me* is one of the most inspiring books I have read in a long time. I was transported along with Carolyn on a journey of faith into the jungles and deserts of the Third-World mission field. While I loved the stories of miracles, of struggles and triumphs, it was the revelations she received from God that I will treasure most. This is a book you should read with your notebook beside you to record the truths she has learned through paying the price of obedience to the call of God. It will change you forever."

—Scott Farhart, MD, author of *Intimate and Unashamed: God's Design for Sexual Fulfillment* and *The Christian Woman's Complete Guide to Health*

"It has been my privilege to be the pastor of Carolyn Figlioli for more than ten years. I can testify that Carolyn is a person of devout faith that drove her from the comforts of America to a life of brutal sacrifice in Africa. In her book, *Follow Me*, she describes her adventures, experiences, and sacrifices since visiting Africa in 2007. Her message comes from a pure heart and a life completely devoted to the service of Jesus Christ. You will enjoy *Follow Me*."

—John C. Hagee, Founder and Senior Pastor of Cornerstone Church, San Antonio, Texas, President and CEO of John Hagee Ministries, Founder and National Chairman of Christian's United For Israel, and bestselling author of *In Defense of Israel, Can America Survive?, Financial Armageddon,* and many other titles

"*Follow Me* is an amazing book charting one woman's courageous journey from the depths of brokenness to her destiny—the heart of God. In her desperate hunger to hear the heartbeat of Jesus, Carolyn dared to step beyond the comfort and familiarity of her daily life and embraced the excitement and challenges of learning to live and love in a vastly different culture.

"Carolyn's story reminds me of my own call to the slums of Asia and through the garbage dumps of Africa, where the Lord taught me about His Kingdom through the children and the poor. I learned about dependence, true hunger, meekness, and mercy. The poor of this world taught me about the true riches that belong to those who are poor in spirit. To this day they remain some of my greatest heroes and professors of love.

"In her passion, Carolyn left behind everything, and her priceless reward, like mine, was encountering Jesus Himself in the faces of some of the most broken and destitute of this world.

"Carolyn's book is a wonderful encouragement to the body of Christ to live in the simplicity of abiding in the ceaseless love of God and loving our neighbor as ourselves. There are no limits to what Jesus can do, even through one little life that is fully laid down.

"I pray that as you read this book, Jesus will stretch your heart to carry more of His love and open your eyes to see Him in the face of the one you minister to each day, whether across the world or across the street."

—Heidi Baker, PhD, Founding Director of Iris Ministries
and author of *There Is Always Enough, Under His Wings, The Hungry Always Get Fed, The Face of Revival,* and *Mama Heidi*

follow me

follow me

Journey into the Sudan
and into the
Heart of the Father

Carolyn Figlioli

TATE PUBLISHING
AND **ENTERPRISES**, LLC

Follow Me
Copyright © 2011 by Carolyn Figlioli. All rights reserved.

No part of this publication may be reproduced, stored in a retrieval system or transmitted in any way by any means, electronic, mechanical, photocopy, recording or otherwise without the prior permission of the author except as provided by USA copyright law.

This book is designed to provide accurate and authoritative information with regard to the subject matter covered. This information is given with the understanding that neither the author nor Tate Publishing, LLC is engaged in rendering legal, professional advice. Since the details of your situation are fact dependent, you should additionally seek the services of a competent professional.

The opinions expressed by the author are not necessarily those of Tate Publishing, LLC.

Published by Tate Publishing & Enterprises, LLC
127 E. Trade Center Terrace | Mustang, Oklahoma 73064 USA
1.888.361.9473 | www.tatepublishing.com

Tate Publishing is committed to excellence in the publishing industry. The company reflects the philosophy established by the founders, based on Psalm 68:11,
"The Lord gave the word and great was the company of those who published it."

Book design copyright © 2011 by Tate Publishing, LLC. All rights reserved.
Cover design by Shawn Collins
Interior design by Chelsea Womble

Published in the United States of America

ISBN: 978-1-61346-782-4
Biography & Autobiography / Religious
11.12.13

Dedicated to the children of Iris Sudan and Iris Mozambique. You have shown me more about the Father's heart than I could ever know from any book. You have shown me how to love from the secret place in God.

acknowledgments

Jesus Christ, You are acknowledged above all else for giving me my very life. You are my true inspiration and the only reason for this book.

Lestra Gross, you are the one Jesus called to mentor me and bring the Word of God to life in my life, and I am so glad that you answered the call. You should have quit on me so many times, yet you stayed with me through all my mess, and I am ever so grateful. You were my Elijah, who always prayed for me to go higher and do more and to go and get that double portion. It is here! You will always be my spiritual mom. I honor you, and I love you so very much.

Pastor John Hagee, my spiritual father, the shepherd who loves his flock. You always bring the good news of the gospel without compromise. Your messages helped to usher me into the saving knowledge of Jesus Christ. I never even asked for you to support me as a missionary, yet you know where every one of your sheep are, and you saw me in a distant land and still, here, you provide for my ministry. Thank you so much.

CDR, my favorite boss and biggest encourager. You always believed in me and let me run with the baton, even when I didn't think I had it in me. You always knew. Thank you for singing my name all those years. I can still hear you in the halls of the school, and I smile!

Gwynne, my biggest fan and friend. You never grow tired of taking care of me. I have great comfort in knowing that you will always be there for me. I love you, my friend. You and your family are special and precious to me.

Heidi and Roland Baker, for your school of laid-down lovers of Jesus. You have kindled and stirred my passion for the One, Jesus Christ, and the one, the one who sits on the road waiting for someone to stop.

Michele Perry, for allowing me to rest and to grow here in this heavenly place in Sudan with your precious babies. They teach me daily about Jesus's love. I look forward to partnering with you in Sudan for a long time to come, spreading the fire of revival all the way north! Yes, love does have a face. Thanks for helping to reveal His love to so many.

Vivian, you are the captain of a multitude of warriors, formed and ready for prayer, all of whom I could not do this without. I have peace and rest knowing that you have my back while I go forward in the battle for souls. I love you, my friend and fellow soldier.

Wendy, my refreshing and lighthearted friend who can always make me laugh. You bring me such joy. I thank God that you are also my prayer partner and that you speak destiny into my life. We do have such fun together. I love you!

Renate, you introduced me to the Jewish Savior and gave me a rich understanding of our heritage in the Jewish people. I bless you, Jerusalem, and I will not be silent concerning you, and I pray for your peace and prosperity. Thank you, Renate, for being my spiritual mom and keeping my lamp burning with precious oil.

Donis, thank you for keeping me healthy. You are priceless, my friend. Even though I don't like to take my vitamins, you have made me realize their importance here in the bush, and I now walk with renewed energy and perfect health. Thank you for keeping my health at the forefront of your ministry to me. I love you.

Zack and Priscilla for your friendship and for speaking such amazing destiny into my life and for always making sure my tummy is full of the best Indian food anywhere! I love you guys!

Susan, my sister, my friend. I love you and am so very proud of you. I love having Orange Leaf with you! And you make the most beautiful babies.

Arlene, my little girl, my lil' sis, the one who handles all my stuff when I am away. You are so precious and priceless to me. I have such peace knowing that you care for everything there on my behalf while I am here. I love you, my daughter, my sister, my friend!

Lola, I will always praise God for the day that you found me on the street with my luggage in hand. You saved my life and gave of yourself to help me become who I am today. You always saw the good in me and who I could become. I am ever so grateful. I love you, friend.

Grandpa, you are my hero. You accepted me as your granddaughter from the start, when I came in off of the street. You introduced me to my Savior and forever planted the seed of who I have now become in Christ Jesus. I love you both so much.

Candice and Pepper, my sweet lil' sisters, two bigger hearts cannot be found. You are my cheering squad and I yours. I am so proud of who you have become. Thank you for calling me sister and loving me as you do. I love you both so much.

Logan, Kaylan and Dylan, and Christian, my nieces and nephews, you guys are my joy and my light. You have such pure hearts and sweet spirits. God has such great plans for you, and I know that you will bring Him glory all the days of your lives. I speak blessings over you and the good that you put your hands to. I love you, Aunt Carolyn.

John and Michael, my brothers who always protected me and kept me from harm. My gentle giants, you are loved by me and by the One who gives you rich life, Jesus Christ.

table of contents

foreword

I arrived in South Sudan in 2006 with little more than the promises of God. In the last five years, I have seen Him stand behind His Word in supernatural, amazingly practical, and extravagant ways. I came with no plan B. Either God was God and He would perform His Word, or I was toast. Raw faith and a bit of holy audacity so often unleash the realm of the miraculous. Our impossibilities are His invitations.

In the first few months, our family of children rescued from trash heaps, brought out of some earth's most desperate circumstances, exploded in size. God did in months what some had labored for years to see. I had people knocking at my door wanting to know my strategic plan. "Ma'am, please give us your strategy. You must have one."

I told them I didn't. They refused to believe me.

The same visitors kept knocking on my door wanting the strategy. Finally I asked Jesus what to tell them because they would not believe all this growth just "happened." I learned something that day. I do have a strategy. Would you like to hear it?

Three little steps to Kingdom success:

1. Every day, wake up.
2. Ask Jesus to show you what He is doing.
3. Go join Him.

Two simple words to embrace all that you are created for: Follow Him.

My journey to my adopted home in Africa did not start with getting on a plane across the world. It started with saying yes to Jesus and falling in love with Him. All journeys that truly matter begin deep inside of us.

Carolyn's story is a demonstration of the profound grace of Jesus and what happens when you fall so in love with Him you will go anywhere and do anything. Her journey started with a dangerous word: *yes*. And this yes-cry of abandonment in her heart led to a yes-walk lived out every day in her life.

She is a demonstration of the goodness of God, who loves us past our past, past our pain, and into our destiny. Her journey shows how our greatest obstacles can become stepping stones when we follow Him. A simple yes can lead you off of the paved road to unknown paths that just might change nations with the power and love of Jesus. It is an honor to have her as part of our Iris Ministries Sudan family.

I pray as you read her story you will be compelled by His amazing love to step off of the paved road into the adventure that comes with radically following His lead. I pray His incredible grace would surprise you, take you on a love journey with Him, and that your world will never be the same. I pray that as you dare to yield to His goodness you too would be swept into the romance of eternity and you would find yourself one of those who dare to follow the Lamb wherever He goes.

—Michele Perry,
Director of Iris Ministries South Sudan
and author of *Love Has a Face*

introduction

Africa has captured my heart. The people, the smells, the sights, the presence of God here; they have changed the tapestry of my life, and this is my story, my journey with God, and with the people of this vast continent. My journey will take you into the interior of at least two nations in Africa, sometimes far out into the bush, and introduce you to the people I have called friends along the way. My story is just that, my story. I have been drawn to Africa for as long as I can remember. I have watched the great famines in Ethiopia, the wars in Sudan, and I have read about the genocide in Rwanda. I wanted to go to Africa and rescue the innocent children and love them in these faraway places. This was the longing of my heart as a small girl, and it followed me into adulthood.

I have read countless books about missionaries who have gone into Africa, who have seen such amazing miracles and acts of God, and I had such a longing to see this power of God that I had been hearing and reading about for years. I thought to myself so many times, why there and not here in America? Why are people being healed of blindness and deafness and being raised from the dead? What is so different about Africa that I should travel thousands of miles to see the power of God? My story will carry you from the wilds of Mozambique into the rugged interior of Southern Sudan, both of these African nations just coming out of years of civil war. I will not dwell upon the politics of these nations, although politics play an important part in their history.

There are many books available concerning the politics of these nations. It is my desire to reveal to you the love of God, and the power of God as He has revealed it to me.

I want my story to give others hope. There are many who are hearing the call to come to Africa or to go to another nation or even to their own neighborhoods in the West, yet they feel that they are not qualified. I want my story to speak to you and to encourage you and to tell you that I was not qualified. I came because God asked me to come. I had to follow my heart and trust God to make the way for me, even in my weakness of faith sometimes. Whether you answer the call in your neighborhood or across the sea to another nation, this story will inspire you to take one step at a time, looking at what is right in front of you and not worrying about the big picture, and learning how to trust God, knowing that He is always looking out for your best interests.

This book was written from the small confines of my tent and from a small room in the center of a children's village that I have called home for almost two years, deep in the heart of South Sudan. I have had to fight scorpions and flies and mosquitoes and gnats in a battleground over my keyboard. I have survived attacks against my health and my body by flesh-eating spiders and flesh-eating bacteria. I have fought bats in latrine holes, negotiated wild dogs on early morning runs before temperatures reached 127 degrees, and traversed swamp-like mud expanses, slip-sliding my way across a flooded plain in order to testify to God's faithfulness. Truly, He will never leave you. I know this from experience. I followed God through all of this because I knew He would see me through to victory, and I want to encourage you to follow Him, and He will show you great and mighty things that you did not know.

awakening of faith

I grew up the daughter of a US military father and a German mother who immigrated to the USA in 1963, when my father returned from duty overseas. We grew up in places like Germany, the Panama Canal Zone, Colorado, Utah, California, and Texas. As a military family, we never stayed in one place long enough to make any lifelong friends. I had four siblings, and I grew up in a very dysfunctional home. Both of my parents drank heavily and there was rarely a weekend where there was peace in the house. For many years, as an adult, I did not even celebrate holidays because of the bad memories I had as a child. I dreaded holidays. An argument or fight always ensued, sometimes bringing the police to our door in the night. I was shuttled back and forth, like luggage, between my parents' home and my fraternal grandparents. Although my grandparents loved me, I never felt like I belonged anywhere so I grew up a shy and nervous child.

I was sexually and mentally abused most of my childhood, from the age of four until I finally left home at fifteen. Twice, I was removed from my parents' home by the authorities for my own safety. I grew up in fear of strangers, in fear of the dark, in fear of my parents, and in fear of constant nightmares.

By the age of fourteen, I was drinking alcohol and smoking cigarettes and marijuana, and I began to pop speed and dabble in cocaine. I ran away from home three times, the third being final. I didn't do drugs or run away to be rebellious. I ran to escape the dysfunction of my family. I had many thoughts of suicide, and I finally left home for good when I was fifteen years old.

At eighteen, I joined the United States Navy, and I started to drink and party even more. I became sexually active and embarked on a journey to find that perfect love and acceptance that had been eluding me all of my life. I wanted someone to love me unconditionally. I was married briefly to a wonderful man who did love me, but because of the excess baggage from my past that I was dragging with me, I played a part in causing it to fall apart due to my selfishness.

I eventually retired from the military and began a career in public education, teaching high school Navy Junior Reserve Officer Training Corps cadets the finer points of leadership and military history. Up until this time I was a radical partier and a radical adventurist. I loved living on the wild side, riding fast motorcycles, jumping out of airplanes, diving the depths of the ocean, driving fast boats, and living the fast life. I searched and searched for that thing that would satisfy me. It remained so elusive, and no matter what I did or where I went, there was something on the inside of me that would never be satisfied. I was driven to quench this thirst, but I didn't know how.

Although my siblings and I attended a Catholic church for much of our childhood, I never really knew God. As a young girl, I used to wonder where He was when I was in such darkness. I used to wonder why we went to church to pray to a God who never heard my prayers, who never rescued me from the terror of the night. I felt like God was this big angry God who would stare down at me with a magnifying glass and just wait for me to mess up and maybe I was doing something wrong to cause the abuse of my childhood. I never saw myself as going to heaven. I didn't even know what heaven was.

I was so clueless concerning Christianity and God stuff. I think the only Bible story I knew was that Jesus was born to the Virgin Mary, and I might have known about Noah and the flood and Moses and the Ten Commandments. I knew about the Ten Commandments, and I knew I must have broken all of them to be living in the circumstances I was living in as a child. I felt like it was my fault my father was sexually attracted to me when he would come to me in the night. What was wrong with me that God would let this happen? This was my view of God. I spent my life thinking that Hell was my life here on earth and one day, if I was good, I would get to go to heaven.

By the time I was in my second year of teaching, post-military retirement, and ending my thirty-something relationship, I knew something had to change in my life. I had a great job, owned my own home with a swimming pool and all new furniture, and I had a brand-new truck and a motorcycle. I had it all, yet I felt so empty inside. I looked at the sum of my life and wondered, what have I really done with it? There had to be more than working and sleeping and drinking. I felt like there was something more, and I needed to know what it was. I was so tired of numbing myself with alcohol every weekend.

On the day of my thirty-ninth birthday, my life took a drastic turn and was never to be the same again. About six months before this, I decided that maybe I should go to church and explore that avenue of fulfillment. I mean, what could it hurt? I had tried everything else and kept running into the big empty return. So there I was, this Catholic girl with a sprinkling of Baptist, walking into this huge Charismatic church. I blended into the pews among four thousand other Sunday morning worshipers. I figured, in a church like this, I could surely go unnoticed, and if I didn't like it, well, I could just not come back and who would miss me, right?

Well, like a fish to fly fishing, I became hooked. I sat in the pew Sunday after Sunday, listening to these great things about a loving God, and I was mesmerized by the truth of this amazing love. I would roll into church on a Sunday morning still hung over from the night before. And each Sunday I attended, I was more and more drawn to this love and acceptance of God. Finally, on my thirty-ninth birthday, just fifteen minutes before midnight, I looked up at the ceiling as I lay in bed, and I told God, "God, if You are really real, and if there is more to life than this, then show me, and I will follow You." Then, I fell asleep. No bells and whistles or angelic visitations or warm fuzzies. I just fell asleep.

The next day when I awoke, I felt a new sense of purpose to life. I walked away from my life as I knew it. I never smoked another cigarette, quit drinking, walked away from all my party friends, and never looked back. I was suddenly hungry, starved, for more of God. I was unquenchable. I read many books, went to hundreds of conferences and meetings, and still I was hungry, even desperate, to experience the reality of God. I didn't want to just read about Him. I wanted to know Him. I wanted to feel God and know that He heard me when I called. I wanted to do the things that Jesus did. I couldn't understand why He would say that we would do more than even He did and I wasn't seeing it. I was frustrated. I was exactly where God wanted me. He had birthed this passion inside of me to run so hard after Him that nothing else would satisfy me.

I had just read about the Brownsville Revival in Pensacola, and I hopped in my truck on my spring break in 2001, and I drove all the way from Texas to Florida non-stop, chasing after God. I cannot explain how desperate I was for the real deal, the raw power, the overwhelming presence of the living God. Pensacola was amazing, and it made me even hungrier. The week that I was there, all I could do was weep and sob and slobber all over the carpet. I felt such an intense love that it literally overwhelmed me, and all I could do was cry. I had never been so broken yet so filled up with love.

I came back to Texas hungrier. I was almost driven, but I have learned that God does not drive us to do anything. The Holy Spirit just keeps drawing us to Himself, and the deeper we go into Him, the more we will want. One day, I discovered a book, *There Is Always Enough* by Heidi and Roland Baker, and I knew that I had found my desire. I wanted to go to Africa. I had to go to Africa.

It was a seed born inside of me that wanted to burst forth, and I could not contain my hunger and passion to go. Still, God had me wait another three years. I had some things I had to face and deal with on the inside before I went. I still had the issues of my past trying to choke out the hunger that I had for God. God in His kindness and in His mercy took me through the deliverance from rejection and low self-esteem and the lack of trust toward others and brought me into a new place of trust and love.

I am so thankful that He took me through these rough spots before I went to Africa. I still had some residual issues that would later come to the surface, but the major root of them was exposed. When it came time for the final cutting away, I was ready for it. It still pained me, and it was not easy by any means to go through the pruning and cutting, but I never doubted that God loved me and wanted me to be set free, so totally free that nothing would hold me down when the day came for me to step into my destiny in Christ and journey to Africa. Even as I boarded the plane for mission's school, I still felt unworthy to be called to go. I had to really trust God's love for me regardless of the many mistakes I felt I had made.

It was His grace that lifted me up and set my feet in a firm place in Him, although a bit wobbly still. God does not call us or send us because we are perfect and somehow qualified to go. He loves to take the weak and lowly and raise them up to confound the wise of the world. Don't ever think that you have disqualified yourself from His high calling. As long as you get up every time you fall down or stumble, and as long as your heart is right in motive, God will continue to transform you into what you have always been created to be. Just don't quit. Faithfulness is what God is looking for. He will always reward faith. Hebrews 11 is our guarantee of this. Faith is what placed me in position for the journey on which I was about to embark, a journey that would change me forever and change who I began to see myself as in Christ. Come follow me into the unknown, into the heartbeat of the Father. Come see what moves Him.

the journey begins

August 1, 2007, is the day I finally realized a childhood dream come true. When I was a very young girl, around the age of nine or ten, I can remember saying to no one in particular that when I grew up, I wanted to be a missionary in Africa. I had no idea what a missionary did except to help the poor. I just knew that I wanted to go to the wilds of Africa, and I wanted to help people. It was not a dream that I actively pursued. I didn't even know God really. It was a long-forgotten dream by the time I grew up, managing to survive the first forty years of my life. I didn't even remember this dream until I set foot in Africa. Then it exploded on the inside of me, reverberating in my very soul, and I knew that I was finally where I had always been created to be: the remote wilds of Africa.

I visited Iris Ministries in Pemba, Mozambique, and spent two weeks at their Children's Center where they cared for street children and orphans. Before I arrived in Africa that first time, I asked the Lord what He wanted to show me while I was there. What do You want to do in me, God? That was my desire: to let Him have full access to my heart and my thinking. He was about to take me on a journey into the very heart of His Son, into the love of Jesus and His great love for me. I needed to understand and experience this kind of love that didn't require anything of me except to receive it. I knew how to give, but I had a very hard time receiving, and He wanted me to learn how to receive.

I boarded the plane, bound for Africa with great expectation. As we entered the Mozambican airspace, I realized that this was finally becoming real. We landed in Maputo, the capital city, for a quick transfer to another plane. There were no computerized terminals or fancy carousels or friendly hostesses to greet you. We carried our bags down a ladder that was rolled out to the plane. Walking across the tarmac, we were herded into the terminal, and the flight coordinator had to individually write all of our names on a new roster, assigning us new seats, and then he ushered us along to get our passports stamped. No fanfare, no grand welcome, just "Move along please." On the wall above the ticket counter was the Mozambique national ensign, a sickle and an AK47, crossed. Talk about nerve-racking.

Then we flew on to Pemba, where I would spend the next two weeks. The land was dry and brown; actually the dirt was a reddish brown. And they spoke Portuguese of all things! I was excited. We loaded our luggage, not to include mine as it got delayed somewhere in Africa, into the back of a flatbed truck and jumped onboard for the short ride to the Children's Center. The road was paved, and people waved and yelled out to us, "Acuna! Acuna!" I later learned that they call all white people this name, which means, white person.

A few days after arriving in Mozambique, we headed out into the bush. We loaded up the flat bed truck with sixteen people from different countries and all of our gear—sleeping bags and tents and backpacks and generator and sound equipment and food—with barely enough room to move our feet for the pile of gear in the midst of us. There were people from the US, New Zealand, France, England, the Netherlands, Belgium, Maputo, and four local pastors from four different villages. We traveled down a paved road until it ran out; then we hit dirt roads and traveled until they ran out, and then all that was left was a tire track trail. We actually ran out of road and went into the bush-bush.

We were so far away from any city that electricity was a foreign concept. It seemed that every star that God had ever flung into the heavens was visible out there. The sky was so vast and limitless, like a thick blanket covering the earth for the night, and the stars were like thousands of diamonds sprinkled over every inch, taking their place to declare the glory of God in all His majesty. I sat in my tent reflecting upon that first day. When we arrived in the village, the first thing I noticed was that almost every child was coughing or had a runny nose. They were covered with flies, in their eyes and mouths, and their bellies were extended with worms and parasites and malnutrition.

Many of the people had open festering sores on their bodies, which I later learned was scabies, usually from a lack of citrus and just being dirty. There is an extreme shortage of water in the bush, and the villagers had to fill many, many containers, which they call jerry cans, with water and carry them back, sometimes for miles, to their village. Water is very scarce, and there are few wells or cisterns. Once a well has dried up, they have to walk many miles to find another watering hole.

The children were cautious of us. We were the first westerners this particular village had ever seen. This village had yet to hear the gospel. We brought out the cameras, and that was the end of their timidity! We would take a picture, then show them, and they would laugh and laugh with joy and amazement. Then we would take another, and they would wave their hands in front of the camera, and I had to explain by sign language not to wave their hands like that. They didn't understand, and so I showed them that they were blocking their faces because their hands were there. They got the idea. I also filmed video and showed them. The expressions on their faces were priceless. They did not speak any Portuguese or English, so we had no common language. They spoke their local dialect, which is Makua. At first this was a challenge to us, but we soon learned that the language of love was universal.

I taught them how to play hopscotch and pick-up sticks. They liked pick-up sticks, so much so that even the grown men insisted on playing. They would laugh at my comments of, "Uh oh!" when they made a mistake. Their sing song voices mimicked mine saying, "Uh oh!" back to me. It was so funny, and I smiled so much that my face hurt. I had now left a legacy of the word "uh-oh" in a remote African village, and that just makes me laugh that this is what I left them with; this and pick-up sticks made out of pieces of hay.

The children stuck to us like glue. Every time we showed them something new, they crowded in so close that you literally could not move. They had no concept of forming a line or staying back so that all could see. It was a clamor to see who could get there first and get the closest, even to shoving the littlest ones out of the way.

There were little girls and boys with their tiny baby brothers or sisters strapped to their backs with a kapalana, which is a wrap that goes about their body as a dress or baby carrier. These children were four, five, and six years old and were carrying little babies that were only months old. I was amazed at how good they were with them. There were also many young mothers who were probably only fourteen or fifteen years old.

The women in Mozambique, and most of Africa, have no reservations about breastfeeding in full view of everyone. Some mothers walk around with their breasts out, ever ready for that hungry infant. This part of the body is not considered sexual. It is, although, very inappropriate to show your knees or thighs or even the outline of them. Our attire consisted of one of the local kapalanas or a long skirt with a shirt while the men wore longer shorts or pants.

After dark, we set up our generator and showed the villagers a worship video of some African people in a modern city singing in their language; they were in awe. They just stared at the video. Some old women even started dancing and swaying with a few of us westerners to the music. It was short-lived because the generator broke after two songs. So we preached a salvation message by flashlight through our one interpreter. Many received Jesus as Savior at the end, and we prayed for many more. Some of the boys tried to press their lower bodies against us in a sexual manner, but we got smart real fast. We just moved to the outer edge of the crowd and continued to pray for them, keeping our hands firmly on their chests to keep them at a respectable distance. We noticed that many older men and women smelled of alcohol, but they still wanted prayer and were very respectful toward us. I later learned that the local alcohol is brewed from maize corncobs and husks and sugar.

I felt such passion as I prayed for these people, an urgency that they know Jesus, really know Him, and that they be healed by His hand. The next day we would have to fix the generator because we were supposed to show the Jesus movie. I was glad though that God changed our agenda, and we let Holy Spirit move the way He wanted to that first night.

I was awakened the next morning by an unexpected problem. It is a natural part of life for a female, but when you are in the bush, in the middle of literally nowhere, an unexpected problem can mean disaster. The same thing happened to another lady. Being that it was unexpected, we were totally unprepared. I knew that this was just another test. I had been taken so far out of my comfort zone in just this last week, starting with my luggage being lost, and me having to go into the bush with the little that I did have.

I was also sharing a tent with a total stranger because she forgot to pack hers, sleeping face to face basically because the tent was so small. God gave me so much grace for this alone, knowing my aversion to sleeping so intimately close to a stranger. We were also just fifteen yards from the pit-latrine and a hog pen. I was actually serenaded awake in the mornings by their snorting and wheeing and grunting. The camp cook-spot was right outside the bamboo wall of the latrine, allowing everyone to see me going in and out twenty times a day because of this new problem. Hey, this is reality here. And as soon as I got out of my tent, I was being thoroughly watched, my every movement, by the village people. Can you say paparazzi? Grace Lord, grace, grace!

Thus my second day in the African bush began. In the morning, we tried to pass out balloons, and were overtaken by clamoring children. We tried to take more pictures—same thing. We tried to hand out orange slices—same thing. We couldn't teach them to wait their turn, that they would all get something. They just couldn't understand that concept. They would clamor and fight until they shoved their way to the front. We would then put everything away until they settled down. We learned to give only when they didn't realize we were giving.

I drank water from a tree vine called a charuba vine. It tasted just like water, although it was thick and sticky looking, with the consistency of boiled okra slime. It still tasted clear and fresh. We also saw a huge African bird that the children kept calling "umpicha." In Portuguese, the word for "one" is *um*. I thought the children were saying, um pitcha, one picture, take one picture. I took many, and they kept saying it. I soon learned through our interpreter that their name for this bird was really umpicha. It was a good laugh, and a word I'll never forget at least.

When I got home to the US, I checked the Internet for this bird, and it is called the African ground hornbill. It is large and black, with a big red ball hanging from its beak. It is very cool looking. It flies and sits in trees. It is about two and a half feet tall and makes a funny guttural noise. This bird is also an endangered bird, and it is rare to see them; so I was thankful for this experience.

That night we showed the Jesus film. The whole village, and those close by, came to watch it. The film was in their Makua language, and they were transfixed. It was the first time most had seen a motion picture. We worked on the generator all morning and into the afternoon; it would not start. The guys called everyone over to lay hands on it and to pray hard. Many of the men of the village were standing right there watching us and probably wondered what we were doing, yelling (praying in earnest) at a machine. It is so funny when I think back on it, wondering what they must have thought. We prayed with all that we had and prayed and prayed and pulled on that cord and pulled on that cord, at least fifty to sixty times, and nothing happened. Finally, we decided that if God wanted us to show the movie, then He would get it to start; and we walked away.

Just then, a couple from another village showed up. The lady had a hideously infected wound on her entire calf area, and they came because they heard there were white witch doctors (assuming we were them) that could heal them. Some of the team began praying and cleaning the wound with some hand sanitizer someone had and some water. Many of the local villagers were crowding so close to watch that it was too hard to work with her, so a team member lifted her in his arms and carried her inside a nearby hut.

Another team member and I were standing close by within the circle of where our tents were stationed. There were drums continuously being beaten in the background somewhere, which was more than likely the local witchdoctor as this is their forte. The men of the village and some of the older boys, about fifteen of them, were standing in a semi-circle around our tents with their arms crossed, a stony, cold look on their faces. Something didn't feel right about the whole situation. The other lady looked at me and asked, "Did you feel the atmosphere shift?" and I agreed that it was not good at all. So she and I got in our tent and we began to do spiritual warfare by praying. About ten to fifteen minutes later, we looked out, and most of the men had dispersed; situation normal, praise God.

The team members who were with the couple came over and said that the lady had on a witch doctor's necklace, meaning that she tried to get healing from one. Our team member asked her to remove it. She did and she also received Jesus as Lord and Savior. Another little girl with an extended belly also had one of these necklaces on. We told the mother that it was making her little girl sick, and could we cut it off and pray for her? She said yes. All of this happened in the space of about an hour or so.

The team leader called us together, and the villagers were still watching us intently. We then gathered as a team to pray, and we just started worshiping and getting lost in Jesus' love. We were praying and singing in the spirit and thanking Jesus for what He had done and what He was going to do that night. We were in this place for about a half hour or so, and when we stopped, we opened our eyes and almost everyone was gone. One of our guys decided to walk over to the generator to see if it would work, and he pulled the cord. It started on the very first pull! After trying all day long, it started and it ran all night. Jesus did it just in time!

It seemed that the whole village heard it, and they came out in force, a huge crowd, to watch the movie. Many more received Jesus as Lord and Savior. We prayed for many, many people and believed that they were touched, because we didn't have inter-preters, so we had no verbal testimony. We prayed for an old woman who had a big saucer ornament in her lip. She was miss-ing an eye in the right socket and both eyes were glued shut by this gook stuff that was coming out of her eyes. They were stuck together, so we wiped them off as best we could with a tissue while we prayed over her. We prayed with her a long time, and still she couldn't see a thing. I told her to come back in the morn-ing for church and we would continue to pray for her.

The next morning we got up at about 5:30 a.m. and loaded everything up before breakfast. The previous day the men on the team and the village men cut bamboo for the new church they were going to build for all the new converts. They also cleared some ground to build it on. We decided that instead of having church we would pray over the land and the people as we walked it out. We prayed and walked a bit, and then we noticed that three people were being led up to us, one of them being the old woman who had arrived earlier with the blind gunk filled eyes. They wanted prayer. One was an old blind man. The other was an old woman who could not lift her left arm or bend it at all.

We gathered around and laid hands on them and prayed. We prayed and waited and prayed and waited, just soaking them in the Father's love. We prayed for a good while, over all three of them at the same time, just soaking them with love and prayer, no hurry, very peaceful. We also asked the blind man and blind woman to rinse their eyes with water. We poured three handfuls for each of them and they washed their eyes three times. We prayed on. I could see the desperation in the man. He was leaning in, and his right hand was in a fist as if he could take hold of Jesus Himself.

Finally, our team leader said, "Hold up. Wait." He held out two fingers to the old man and asked, "How many?" The old man held up two fingers! The team leader backed up and held out four fingers and asked him how many. The old man held up four! By this time, tears were rolling down my face in utter amazement at God's goodness. The team leader moved further and further away, and he could still count them! My silent tears still came as I repeatedly exclaimed the name of Jesus in my excitement! Tears of amazement were also coming from the old man's eyes. I was beside myself and so overjoyed and amazed. Jesus did it! Jesus did it! Jesus made the blind man see!

The blind woman said she could see better! She could see better! Oh my gosh, the scripture fulfilled! The blind see! The woman with the arm mobility problem then was asked to lift her arm. She tried and winced in pain; she couldn't. We noticed two witch doctor necklaces around her throat and we asked her to remove them because they were stopping her healing. She seemed reluctant at first. It was as if she had to think about it. Should she really trust this "new" medicine, and would it really work for her? After some consideration, and I think seeing the blind eyes open, she removed her necklaces. We prayed again for a few minutes and then asked her again to lift her arm. She lifted her arm high to the heavens, and the look on her face was priceless! She had the biggest smile, the biggest eyes, and her lips were trembling in such gratitude and amazement at our great God. Jesus showed up at the last hour in power! Our preaching was not without power. Signs and wonders followed, and many came to Jesus that weekend.

I learned as we were leaving that the name of this village is "Cho'ver" (pronounced show-vare), which means rain. What a prophetic name and picture! Let it rain! The glory of heaven rained on this village that day. Only Jesus, only Jesus! I learned so much from that first outreach. I noticed that we were never in a hurry with our praying and our worship. Most times we would just stay and soak the people with love who needed healing. Every time we prayed before each event, we never had just one person praying for that event. We would all lift up our own prayers in one accord. Each voice was just as full of passion and each heart was just as enflamed as the other so our focus was never on one person's voice. Our focus was on the One.

When we prayed together, out loud, all of us, each in our own prayer language, having a personal communion with God, we were not listening to someone's voice or words and focusing on it. The person being prayed for does not have to understand or agree or even hear (deaf people don't hear) in order to receive the healing. The blind man was standing there with his fist clenched, and he didn't move or leave or seem confused at what to do next. He just stood there and waited until he could see! He had no clue what we were doing. He just knew we were doing something, and he was willing to stand there until the sun went down if that is what it took. He didn't understand a word we said. Only heaven needs to hear your prayers, God says. We all have a part in bringing the rain.

Most of the time, we would pray in the spirit, using our gift of tongues that Paul talks about in 1 Corinthians 14, letting the Holy Spirit lead the way. Prayer was never a chore or something we had to stir ourselves up for. It just happened. We traveled six hours in the back of a truck over rough roads, yet we would erupt in praise and worship and blast each other with prayer, not even aware of the road ahead of us. The Holy Spirit would come, and we got in the river. We would sing for miles and not ever sing the same song twice. We lived in the river that weekend. We didn't live in the circumstances and problems around us.

I was learning about being humble and meek and about God's amazing grace. So much had happened to cause me to lay down pride and self-comfort. The biggest hurdle for me was using the latrine with only a thin layer of bamboo standing between myself and the rest of the people in the camp. Laying down all fear and just going, knowing that there were millions of maggots in that hole and roaches all around it. Also being in the same dirty clothes for three days and even sleeping in them and not showering for five days, was so totally out of my character.

I also learned that I could get used to any smell. I had a very sensitive nose and couldn't stand the smell of unclean bodies or bad breath or anything offensive to my nose. How would I be able to stand all the smells? After a while, I smelled worse to myself than any of the villagers smelled to me. I was surprised at how I got so used to the smell of Africa. I even smelled my things when I got home to the USA and found that I missed that smell! How weird is that? I craved that smell because that smell is what God loves, and that smell is where God came down and touched my heart to the core. I could smell God. I also noticed that when we left the village, there were very few kids coughing and sick. The presence of God permeated that village and brought healing.

Our trip home was glorious and full of joy as we rejoiced in all that God had done in the village of Cho'ver. When I finally returned to my room back at the Children's Center, there sat my lost luggage. I was so excited, and I immediately went in search of clean underwear. I started tossing things everywhere, frantic to find them so I could get a nice shower. My underwear weren't there! They were missing, all of them, among other things. Every single pair was gone. How crazy is that? So now I was living for three weeks with three pair of underwear, doing laundry every other night, by hand of course. I will admit that I was a little upset, but I also knew that this test would unfold even more amazing things that were far worthier of my time than worrying over stolen underwear. I had really lost all of my comfort zone by then, and I would gladly have given all I had at that time for more of the heart of God! It was an amazing first trip to Africa, and I learned so much while I was there for that short time, mostly about how much God loves everyone and desires to see none perish. I knew that I would return as soon as I could the following year. And I knew that the heart of the Father was already nudging me to love the poor with all that I had. The call to Africa was already being planted as a tiny seed. I was hearing that still small voice.

the calling

It was during my second visit to Africa in the summer of 2008 that I visited Maputo, which is in the south of Mozambique. It is a fairly modern city with electricity and running water in much of the city. Our team visited a place called Bocaria, which was the city garbage dump. I went with a small team from Iris Ministries to visit the church in the dump and to pray for those wanting prayer who lived up on top of the dump. As we drove in, my eyes were as big as nickels. There was a mountain of garbage which had been collecting in mass for years. There were layers and layers reaching at least thirty feet high, and I am guessing that it covered the size of maybe ten football fields. When we went up on top, there were small groups of people scattered all over this massive field of trash. There were fires burning, the smoke hanging heavy in the air, along with the smell of rotten garbage and human waste. Small children were running all over in bare feet among thousands of pieces of broken glass. They were picking through the garbage looking for something to eat.

I was in shock I think, speechless. When we went up to the first person to pray, I thought to myself, "What can I offer these people? I have no idea what to pray for them?" I felt helpless. But we prayed anyway, squatting down in the trash with them, hundreds of flies on us as we prayed. I was so moved by the plight of these people that I didn't even care about the flies. At one point, as I looked out over this scene, I just started to weep. I was so broken for these people that I couldn't even speak. Then, off in the distance, I saw a large flock of about seventy pure white birds soaring over this dump, and I felt like the Lord was reminding me that He doesn't forget His people and that His Spirit was there, even in that place, for all who would receive. The tears kept coming.

Then some man came up with his friend who appeared to be about sixty years old. He said that he had been trying for ten years to get his old friend to receive Christ, but he wouldn't and would we pray for him. I said only one thing to this precious old man, "What do you have to lose?" And then I just laid my hand upon his heart and asked Jesus to touch him there. I just kept my hand there and didn't say another word. Then the old man became agitated and started to motion that his heart was beating fast. He said that something was moving upon his heart and that he couldn't explain this feeling except that it must be from God. He had never been moved like this, and he wanted to receive. He received Jesus! Just like that, just a few words, just a gentle touch, he received the love of God. His Son came to meet this man in the garbage dump.

Our team leader then told us that it was time to go. As we were about to leave, there was a bulldozer very near to us, pushing trash into a heap. The people around were getting very agitated, and I thought that maybe they hadn't had a chance to pick through the trash and were upset that it was already being bulldozed. Our team leader, when I asked him if that was the reason, told me that it was not. He was hesitant to tell me more. Then he said, "There is a dead baby in there." My mouth dropped, and I said, "We have to do something!"

I ran over to the pile of garbage and I started sifting through the trash, and there he lay, a newborn baby with the umbilical cord still attached. I reached in and lifted him out of the trash and he was still soft in my hands and there was residual blood in the tiny crevices of his perfect little fingers and toes and he looked to be about two months premature. My tears poured down upon him as I held him close and I prayed for God to raise him back to life. I had never in my life felt such pain and such helplessness. I cried out to God, "God, what am I supposed to do with this?" And I wept like a baby for this still and lifeless baby, so perfectly made.

Within a couple of minutes, our team leader said that we had to go because it wasn't safe there anymore. The people were becoming more agitated. I couldn't lay this baby boy down in that trash heap again. Through my tears, I asked him to find something to wrap him in at least. He found a perfect little piece of clean cloth in the midst of the trash pile. We wrapped him gently, and I laid him back down with such a heavy, heavy heart. Our leader said that he would come back to give him a proper resting place.

He took me by the shoulders, lifted me up, and literally led me away. I wept. He stopped me and said he wanted to pray for me. He laid his hand upon my heart and prayed, "Thank You, Lord, for this lady who loves my people so much. Bless her and heal her heart." My feet felt like lead weights, and my heart felt heavier. I wasn't even looking where I was going. I was wrecked in my heart and soul, undone.

We went into the little church at the bottom of the garbage heap, and I was asked to speak, to bring the message. It had been like that this entire trip. I had been asked many times, for no obvious reason, to preach the message. I thought, *I cannot possibly do this now, not after what I have just experienced*. But I did. I just leaned into the Holy Spirit and let Him guide my heart and my mouth to move in time with His. I remember that I spoke about living the dream that God plants into our DNA from the time of our creation. He knows the plans that He has for us, and He forms our personality according to our DNA, that is what hones us in to this plan if we follow His leading.

I told the people of that church about my lifetime of wrong choices and bad decisions and how even after all of this, I was still walking out the plan that God had all along for me. After church, as we were getting ready to leave, and I looked out across the expanse of the garbage dump, I received a revelation of the end time wedding feast. These people knew they were hungry, and they would come to partake of the living Bread when He was offered. His wedding feast is when His people are hungry enough to enjoy the Bridegroom and still hunger for more of Him. The hungry would always be fed. Will we partake, or will we be too busy with our cell phones, with our computers, with our jobs, with our lives? He is looking for the hungry to come. He was calling me.

For the next two days, I began wrestling with God. He was clearly calling me to full-time missions, and He was doing a work in my heart and revealing His heart for me as my Father. I had never understood a father's love until this trip. And I met my Father there. I was the one who kept wrestling with my thoughts and with my western security. Even after that first trip to Africa, I came home declaring that I could never be a full-time missionary! I could never live in such harsh conditions. God didn't wrestle back. He just held on to me, tight. Day and night for those two days, I could think of nothing but His voice calling me, that still small, gentle voice, asking, "Will you go, Carolyn? Will you go for Me, just for Me? Will you follow Me?"

I kept thinking of that baby in the trash heap, and I looked at the "human condition," and how so many people, all over the world from every walk of life were living in virtual trash heaps, their lives a mess of broken hearts and tossed out dreams and the stench of sin. He was calling me to go to those living in these places, wherever He might send me, to the very poor. And I finally said, "Yes, Lord, I will go." And he asked me to sell everything that I had and give myself to the poor, the poor in spirit, the poor in heart, the broken and wounded, to give all of me for Jesus, not for the poor but for Him.

It was there at Bocaria that I understood the wedding feast and Jesus's love for His bride, just as we are, in our human condition. I saw the banqueting table atop the dump. People were starving, and they knew Jesus was their food. He was the feast, and as I gazed upon that place and His beauty there, love looked back at me, and I was undone. I had nothing to offer that baby and that precious old man except the deepest rending of my heart and a love that I never knew existed in me, Jesus's love.

At that moment, I wanted more than anything else in the world to be naked and poor and hungry, and I wanted for nothing but Jesus. I wanted to be in the dying place, in the dirt, in the dump, where the only thing that mattered was this heart-wrenching love poured out.

It wasn't until the following year that I went to Iris Ministries Harvest Mission's School in Mozambique, but while I was there I met a little girl in the Children's Center who was always so sad. She was about three years old, a very frightened little girl who arrived about two months previous. Her mommy went to prison, and in many parts of Africa, if a mother goes to prison, and there is no family left to care for the children, the children also go to prison. If no one comes to bring food, they starve or rely on someone's mercy. Conditions are horrible, and there is sexual and physical abuse. They don't receive medical care, and they might receive one meal a day. The mother begged the Iris Children's Center to take her baby and care for her until such a time as she could be released from prison.

When I looked into this little girl's eyes I saw such deep sadness there. They were the eyes of so many children in Africa who found themselves as orphans or abandoned, to take whatever love they could in a world of broken trust and shame. This made me think of the many children even in the west who found themselves orphans because of these same circumstances. Many children all over the world are left orphans because of the poor choices of their parents. This is just another part of the human condition that affects the lives of so many. God says to care for the widows and the orphans. Many orphans are thrown in the trash heaps while their parents are still alive, children such as these.

After many days of winning this little girl's trust, one morning I was able to sit on the ground and have a breakfast roll and tea with her, and for the first time, she laughed. I ran and chased her, scooped her up and tickled her, and she was happy and laughing in that small piece of time. Every day after that I went to play a bit with her. I took her to church with me and held her and loved her. I wanted her to know that she was not abandoned. I visited her mother in prison and prayed with her and I could tell that the mother loved her little girl very much. I brought pictures that her baby girl had colored and told her that her little girl was happy. This brought the mother some peace. Both of these precious souls needed to know that the Father loved them and had not abandoned them. He sees the mess of our lives, the human condition, and He cares. It's up to us to take the Father's love to these who find themselves in the trash heaps of life.

It took a trash heap to awaken my heart to my calling from God. You may not have a Bocaria Garbage Dump where you live in your city, but I can guarantee that there are many trash heaps to be found where people are waiting for the trash to be bulldozed so that they can find something usable in their lives. It only takes a caring person to help them sort through the rubble and find the true life that was first placed within them before death came to steal it away. There is a dying world living in the trash heap. Jesus sees it as a place to hold His wedding feast, a place where His living Bread can be offered, the Bread of life. It was in the trash heap that He was calling me to come.

I knew I was in for some testing and pruning and growing, and I knew that God would be gentle as He took me through it. I knew I had to go lower still in order to experience God the way I needed to know Him. I also knew that I was hungrier than ever before for His very presence in my life. I went to Africa that first summer, and I returned and nothing in my life changed. I was still the same me, and I actually battled even more against my flesh. Something needed to change, mainly me and my circumstance, or I would die spiritually. I was dry, and I was thirsty, and I had run out of wells. Nothing satisfied anymore. All the conferences and meetings and revivals couldn't penetrate the dryness I felt. This is exactly where God wanted me, in that desperate place where nothing could satisfy but what He had made ready for me all along.

I remember that second trip back to Mozambique so clearly. I pictured the children standing in the line for lunch every day at the Children's Center. Every day the Center would feed all the hungry, the children from the surrounding village. The children were fed every single day, the same food, at the same time, the same amount. It never changed. Every single child was fed. Yet they still fought and pushed and shoved to get to the front of the line. They acted like they were starving and that they might not get anything. The Lord said to me, "These are the poor and the naked and the hungry, and they will be fed. There is always enough. Oh that you would have that same hunger for Me, for you also are poor and naked and hungry. Oh that you would be that desperate to eat at My table, for what I offer day after day. Come if you are hungry, and you also will be fed. There is always enough."

I was undone, because I had spent the last year casually walking after God. I had lost that passion and that burning, and I was desperate to get it back but just couldn't pull it off on my own. I had spent the last year trying to, and it seemed that the harder I tried, the further God seemed from me.

I asked myself many times that summer of 2008, could I endure the dirt, no food, not having help, feeling like I am in it alone? Would I? I felt that there would be no turning back, that this time I would have to face me and commit to what God was calling me to, whatever it might look like. Was I ready? No. Are we ever? God isn't looking for us to be ready; He is just looking for our yes. When we say yes, He makes us ready. My destiny is to become a son of God. My destiny is to become like Jesus and no other. Just be myself and grow with Jesus. Don't fret, don't fear man, don't fear the unknown, just follow Jesus.

This hunger cannot be birthed in my soul. It can only be birthed in my spirit. God increases His Spirit in me when I meditate on Him. He creates my hunger out of that place. He creates my hunger out of the place of rest, His rest. Someone on our team said that he would look at his son, his little toddler son, trying to poop in the potty, and he would have this straining, struggling poop-face. That is sometimes how we "try" to get into the presence and rest of God. We do this poop-face thing when all we have to do is let Him happen. I know He has to laugh at us when we are trying so hard because He loves us so much.

I had never felt more insecure or uncertain than I did in that season. God does not bring confusion or anxiety, but He does allow us to become restless and unsure of ourselves in order to bring us into alignment with His purpose for us and our reliance on Him. Since my first day back in Pemba, I had to face the mountain I had created over the past year. I had been so impatient and so full of myself. Every day, throughout the day, there were situations that tested my patience. I knew this was God doing a work in me and delivering me from myself. So many times I cried out that year, "God, save me from myself!" and I could go no further in my walk until I overcame this.

I was jogging one day, and the Lord said to me, "Carolyn, it's easy to live in the dying place." And the song by Casting Crowns, "Caught in the Middle," kept reverberating in my head for months. "Just how close would I get Lord to my surrender, to losing all control?" Here I had been for the last year, just doing Christianity. I wasn't stepping off the deep end into the raging sea like Peter when Jesus called for him to come. I was afraid. I was afraid of man's rejection if they didn't receive the message of salvation or love or whatever love looked like on any particular day. I was caught in the middle, between really dying and living and comfortable Christianity. It was time for me to step out of the boat into the raging sea, and if I died, then I died. It was time to live in the dying place and lose myself and the things I was holding on to.

I got to preach to big crowds and small groups in Africa. When I finally realized I was preaching to me, it was all about letting go of what I'd been holding on to and living the dream that God put into my DNA before time existed, my dream of Africa. When I finally got quiet enough to be real with myself and with God about what He wanted for me, everything became crystal clear for the first time in my walk with the Lord. I knew my path. I literally asked God, "Where do I go from here, God?" And He answered, "Go to a land that I will show you, and when you get there, I will tell you more."

> This is my journal entry on the last day of wrestling with God over my destiny. This is where I came face-to-face with God and with myself:
>
> My mind runs all over the last five weeks since I have been here and my heart races to catch up and it is torn this way and that, so deeply pierced it's as if my very soul has holes and love is pouring through.
>
> Maybe for once I should really follow my heart. Maybe for once I should follow my dream and not my head and quit being so afraid of what I'm giving up. Maybe what I'm giving up can't even compare to what I will gain.
>
> Maybe I should quit thinking about all of the "hows" and focus on the "who." I find peace and rest here in Africa, the Sabbath rest of God. My soul does prosper here. All of my "Jesus encounters" are through Your people, God. I look into all these faces—the faces of Africa—and I keep saying to myself, I know that these are the faces of God.

I see You in the lady possessed by demons and now set free. I see You in the old man at the dump. I see You in the children of Africa, in all the little faces, even the baby boy laid to rest in the garbage heap. I see You when I look in the mirror. I see the love and the hope that You have for each one of us, in all of humanity, no matter our condition. No wonder Jesus intercedes on our behalf day and night. No wonder the Holy Spirit groans for us. How could You forget even one? I can't. Jesus lives in the place of broken glass and broken hearts and tossed out dreams, and He wants to mend them. There is no place that He can walk and not feel it.

I will go with Jesus, wherever He says go, because I know that there is no place that He sends me where He won't also go with me. I prayed that I would follow my heart, that Jesus would make my heart bigger than my mind, and that love would rule them both.

As my first visit to Africa drew to a close, I left knowing that I would return. It wasn't until a year later that I made the journey back to Mozambique and then heard the clear call of God for my life. I felt the stirrings of God on my heart for this continent, but I was still hesitant to say yes to Him, to leave everything and just go, even though I knew in my heart that He was calling me. I was still too attached to my secure job and all my things and the comforts of modern society to just go and live in the bush. I didn't think I had what it took, so I remained uncomfortably comfortable in all my trappings. Little did I know that this second trip would be so different from my preconceived expectations and that my life would take such a drastic change by the end of that second journey.

I was still waiting on the Lord for a clear word on what direction my life would take. I was still restless inside, and my mind and spirit were ablaze with thoughts of giving my all to these people who were so poor. My flesh was still fighting my spirit though, and I couldn't say yes yet. I was still having a hard time imagining my life without modern conveniences. I laugh now as I look back on this time, but as I lived it, it was a very scary thought to me, and so my flesh was screaming, "No!" while my heart was crying, "Yes!"

I want to encourage all who read this that missions and ministry and missionary are words that apply to every single person who is doing something to advance the kingdom of God. Many people look at missionaries as people who are in the bush of some wild untamed country, pouring out their lives, and risking it all for God. A missionary is someone who is on a mission to advance the kingdom of God, regardless of where it is. A missionary is one who is sent, one who goes, wherever that is.

Just because God has called me to radically alter my life's course, not everyone is called to do this, and I am no better or different than someone who is in the military fighting in Iraq or someone who is ministering in the inner city of Los Angeles or someone who is serving as a daycare worker among twenty-five screaming toddlers or a full-time mother and homemaker. Just the word "homemaker" is a ministry in and of itself. We are all serving in places that require radical adjustments in our lives. Wherever God has placed you in ministry, it is important because God has designed you for that place.

Unless you are called by God Himself to a radical place, then don't go just because you want to or you feel you should. The average lifespan of a missionary serving overseas in a third world country is one year. Eighty-five percent quit after one year. Those who stay the course are usually the ones who have had a very strong word from the Lord to go, and to do anything else would not make sense. When you hear from the Lord to go, then make sure that it is confirmed again and again. When God calls, He usually keeps speaking to you over and over, so you have no doubt that it is Him, if you are listening.

When God is calling you to big things, He will speak loud and clear and it might not always be what you want to hear at the time. When I returned from my second trip to Africa, I asked God where He wanted me to go. I always thought I would go to Mozambique. I mean, I bought the Rosetta Stone Portuguese language CDs, and I was going to learn it so I would be ready!

The only thing that I heard was, Sudan. Sudan! Sudan? You're kidding, God, right? I am scared of Sudan. I have no desire to go to Sudan. Don't You know that they kill people there? This cannot be God. I ignored this still small voice and waited for the "Mozambique" calling. It never came. Just Sudan. After questioning God many times over the next month, I finally said, "If this is You and this is true, then God, give me the desire in my heart to go to Sudan." That was all that God needed to hear from me. That day, I accepted this call and opened my heart to it. Over the next month, my desire for the people of Sudan grew and grew until I could think of nothing else. I wanted to go to Sudan and all fear was gone. I felt such a peace in my soul, and I knew that this was God.

Many of my well-meaning friends were asking me if I was sure and wasn't I scared and, my gosh, Sudan! This was a test, I think, from God to see if I would stay the course and trust His voice. Spiritual leaders and pastors and people that you respect will question you. Welcome their questioning. Listen to their advice. Always listen to the advice of a wise person, but make sure that the final advice that you follow is from God. It is good to have the input of those who love you and want what is best for you, so never shut them out because they "just don't understand." When you do go into the mission field, they will be your biggest cheerleaders and supporters, because you welcomed their questions and respected their advice.

Over the next six months, as I began to sell my new house and furniture and put in my notice with my employer, where I was making really good money, God gave me such peace of mind and heart that I was doing the right thing. I was close to fifty years old and should have been saving for retirement and paying off that house, but God put it in my heart not to worry about my future, that it was His job to make sure it was secure. I felt as if He had restored me as in the days of my youth. I really felt so good physically and mentally. Only God can do that. Even when the home buyer's market in 2009 was at its lowest in a decade, my house sold for what I bought it for three years earlier. The day that it sold and all of my furniture was gone, just hours later, I received my acceptance letter to a mission school that I had been waiting to hear from for almost five months. There are so many amazing testimonies concerning my journey from my calling to my first assignment a year later. All along God kept saying to me, "Trust Me," and like Abraham, I trusted Him.

In May of 2009 I left once again bound for Africa, on my way to Iris Harvest Missions School in Mozambique, knowing that I would never be the same person as I was when I left. I left the USA and many friends and family, not knowing when I would return again. I just knew that I had to follow Jesus. I had to follow the Lamb, and together we would chart the course of the rest of my life.

journey into sudan

After three months of school, I graduated from Iris Harvest Mission School in August 2009 and immediately headed for the Sudan. Leaving behind the lush, rich, cultivated landscape of Entebbe, Uganda, which borders the beautiful Lake Victoria just outside of Kampala, we flew over northern Uganda. The landscape started to change from this rich vegetation to wide open stretches of dirt plains, and then again to dense, dark forests. By the time we came into the Sudan airspace, I could see no sign of modern civilization. Small, round, cone-shaped roofs dotted the landscape as far as the eye could see. I was entering the interior of South Sudan, where civil war had raged for over fifty years, where the Lost Boys of Sudan, thousands of young Sudanese boys, walked across a thousand miles of Sudanese terrain to Ethiopia and then on to West Kenya to escape the war and extreme famine. My mind and heart race with anticipation at what I would encounter there.

Sudan is a very different world than any other place I have visited in Africa. I landed in the town of Yei, which is a three-hour drive on a dirt road from The Democratic Republic of Congo, and about the same distance to the Kaya, Uganda, border. There were no paved roads in all of South Sudan except for the city of Juba. In the deep south, the land is rich and lush, where vegetation grows all year round. There are many fruit trees and vegetables: mango, papaya, coconut, pineapple, avocado, guava, sweet potato, maize corn, onions, tomatoes, okra, yams and ground nuts just to name a few. Although the land produces much, the poverty remains at record levels. When I arrived in 2009 the land had only experienced about three years of peace from the over fifty-year civil war, and yet there was still violence all around.

There is a group that originated in Uganda called the Lord's Resistance Army (LRA), that still raids villages and crops and animals. When this group comes into town, the people leave their fields for the safety of their village center, or a small town. You can read more about the LRA online. Know that they are a very real entity and every day people's lives are affected by this band of raiders. There is much corruption in the country on all levels. Many people were still living under the war mentality, trying to get what they could, while they could get it; even at the expense of other's misfortune.

The people are the most beautiful color of the darkest and smoothest black that I have ever seen on a people. It is the blackest of black, and their features are so angular and chiseled. I think that they are so beautiful and cannot help, even now, to stare at them. I never tire of looking at them. They are a very tall people. The main tribes here in South Sudan are the Kakwa, the Mundari, the Dinka, the Neur, and the Bor. There are other tribes, but these are the ones you hear of the most. They are a proud and fierce people. For many of them, their wealth is shown in the quantity of cattle they have. Their lives revolve around cattle. Cattle are given as bride prices, and if you do not have enough cattle, you do not marry. Cattle are also used in pagan sacrifices. This causes a lot of tribal warfare as one tribe raids another's cattle, killing innocent victims as they are caught in the crossfire. Unlike their forefathers who used spears, many of these tribesmen now use AK47s. It is the weapon of choice.

Just after the peace agreement was signed between the north and south of Sudan in 2006, a disarmament plan was put into effect. There are armories all over to store these collected weapons and ammunitions. There are always stories of tribes raiding these armories to obtain these caches of weapons. It is an endless cycle of arming and disarming, only to be repeated monthly.

On my arrival into Sudan, I first stayed at Iris Ministries Sudan Children's Center and lived in a small camping tent for twelve days as part of a short term outreach team. My first year in Sudan was actually with another ministry full time. I did hear from the Lord that this was His plan for me at that time, so I didn't become a part of the Iris team full time until 2010. The children of Sudan are like children all over the third world. They are happy, they are hungry, they are poor, and they are resilient beyond belief. There are so many stories of children witnessing such acts of violence that you wonder how they can still be happy and seemingly untouched by it all. I have talked with teenagers from the Congo who were rescued from being child soldiers for the rebel army, where girls are only used as sex slaves and as pack carriers and laborers. They were basically taken in the dark of night from their very beds only to be given to a grown man to warm his. Where young boys are forced to kill and mutilate or die a violent death themselves if they refuse. These are young people who have seen more in one year than we can even fathom in a lifetime.

Yet, there in the safety of the Iris Children's Center, they were happy, and they prayed with such passion that it put me to shame that I wasn't as passionate. They truly love Jesus so much here. He is everything to them. The children have so many sad stories, yet they love Jesus and find joy in Him. They have been through hell, yet they smile and love others almost without reservation.

One girl who was three years old watched as her father killed her mother because her father wanted to be rich, and the witch-doctor told him he would have to kill a human as a payment for this special magic. The mother's family was angry, and they retaliated by killing him, leaving the children without parents. Worse, they refused to take care of them after killing the father. And now, there was a little girl who had been tossed out and nobody wanted. I knew already that God was going to take me deeper still on a journey even further into His heart.

Most of the people live in the typical African mud hut with thatched roof and dirt floor. There are no real stores here, only market stalls. A shopping center, or even a small strip mall, cannot be found. If you come into country and don't plan to work, you must bring in whatever money you will need, as there are no ATM machines in South Sudan. You cannot just go to a bank and withdraw money. Credit does not exist in South Sudan. They don't even understand the concept of checking accounts and credit cards. Although South Sudan is one of the poorest countries in the world, it is very expensive to live here. There are no set prices in the market. If you are a westerner, everything is tripled in price, so usually you send a local to the market for you.

As this part of my life began there in this third world country, I still had no idea where my journey was going to take me two weeks down the road. God was keeping me on the Abraham road, only telling me my next step right before it got there. His word to me was, "Go, and then I will show you." And so, I went.

Within days of arriving for my short-term missions trip with Iris Sudan, I embarked upon the most amazing adventure of my entire lifetime. I literally felt like I had stepped into the pages of *National Geographic*. We headed first for the city of Juba. The city population was close to one million and most of them, probably 95 percent of them, lived in huts with metal roofing. Most had no plumbing or electricity. We drove on a dirt road for seven solid hours, which was pitted every mile of the way with bumps, ruts, and potholes. It took us exactly three hours to drive fifty-eight miles, and Juba was one hundred miles away. There were police roadblocks all along the way, and the police and soldiers were all armed with AK47s. If you didn't look the right way or say the right thing, they made you pay to pass. We only had to do that once. We finally got to Juba, and we went to a neighborhood where there was a large Mundari Tribe population. The main tribe lives another fifty miles north, which is where we headed to the next day.

The Mundari Tribe people are cattle herders. They own thousands of head of cattle, 99 percent of the cattle are white, and they do not eat them or sell them. The cattle's sole purpose is to show the tribe's wealth. They collect cattle like we collect cars, houses, and stocks. They only cook one for very special occasions or pay a bride price in marriage or use them for sacrifice to their gods. The Mundari are the second tallest people in Sudan, the Dinka being the tallest. We were greeted by men and women who were on the average six feet tall or taller, most at six-foot-five and taller. They also had these etched scars on their foreheads, where they are marked at a very young age by cutting V-shaped designs into their skin, and as they grow older, they recut to make sure the scars remain. The Dinka cuts are carved straight across, from temple to temple. Although it is not a good thing to do, I think it looks very cool. The different tribes, of course, use their own unique markings, some even looking like raindrops sprinkled across their foreheads.

When we went into the Mundari Tribe's territory fifty miles north, into the county of Terekeka in the village of Lowkwini, we passed many cattle camps. Many young boys, as young as even six or seven years, are sent to these camps to work and live with the cattle. They do not wear clothes. Even the grown men many times do not wear clothes, wearing just a blanket type toga robe, leaving one side of their body exposed. They live, sit, eat, and sleep with the cattle. They walk the herd everywhere they go, and these very large cattle actually *mind* the humans. These cattle are definitely bigger than our Texas longhorns. The cattle are trained so well that they turn right or left with just a word or a clicking sound from the herdsmen.

We arrived in the village, and boys and girls came running to see who we were; the boys being naked. And when we had church, they came naked. Needless to say, that took a little getting used to. The men did wear clothes to church, I am grateful to say! The young men of marriageable age put a thin covering or mask of tan colored dirt on their faces to *attract* the women. I am telling you, I felt like I was transported to a *National Geographic* documentary. I never once felt any fear. It is amazing how much peace you have when you know you are going with God. Because if I didn't go with God and these almost seven foot tall men with painted and cut faces, wearing only a toga-type throw with one side totally open and exposing their body came up to me, I would have been extremely scared.

These gentle giants came and extended their hands in greeting and were so nice. Although we were greeted in a friendly manner, we still felt extreme darkness hanging over that place. As we looked around, we saw that there were these twenty-foot-tall poles planted in the ground about every four acres or so that were painted white and black striped and had one bull horn attached at the top which was also painted. These were the Asherah poles of the Bible. When men wanted to become leaders in the tribe, they had to slaughter a bull, dig a hole, put money, blood, and alcohol in the hole, and then plant this decorated pole as an offering to the gods. Very creepy.

We hadn't eaten since breakfast, so the team went to get something to eat at a roadside stand about twenty minutes away. Three of us decided to stay at this small village church shelter to fast and pray. I was amazed at the peace I had staying there. There were just the three of us skinny, pale women, and God of course, with no car, in the bush with the closest main road twenty minutes away. No one bothered us. In fact, some of the kids stayed to watch us intercede and worship. Then a very large man was led in by a very old woman. He had these huge hands and very large feet and a big head. He was the largest man I had ever seen in person, and it wasn't fat. It was pure largeness. I actually referred to him thereafter as the large man. He sat quietly, never once looking at us, his eyes downcast and constantly moving side to side. His eyes were red, and he hugged his body and fidgeted a lot, and looked like he was sort of possessed by demons, but quietly. Still, we felt extreme peace and totally safe.

Again, it is amazing how all fear is cast out by the perfect love of Jesus. After we had been there for about an hour or so, the old lady wanted us to pray for this large man. We learned that he was blind and had much pain in his body. So we went right over, laid hands on him, and began to pray. After a few minutes, we asked if he could see. My friend Jennie stood about six feet away and held up three fingers. He was able to focus on them and acknowledge this, praise Jesus! She moved farther away, but he couldn't see farther. But all of his pain was gone! At that time, our team came back from dinner, and our service began, well, continued.

After sharing the gospel of Jesus and giving testimonies of His healing power, we prayed for the sick and demon possessed. A small boy was healed of a deaf-mute spirit and was set free to hear and speak! Two babies were instantly set free from burning fevers. Some teenagers came forward with headaches and were instantly set free. There were also salvations. The people who came were small in number, maybe only forty at most, yet God did so much there. It was nightfall by then and too dark to do any more as electricity does not exist in most of South Sudan, so we ended the service. We then pitched our tents in the church, which was open on all sides but one, with a grass roof, tree trunks for pews, and a dirt floor. Our tents fit right in.

It had been raining all day and it was very wet outside. By the way, this village had had no rain in three seasons of planting, about a year and a half, and it rained all day the day we were there, seriously, all day long! Earlier, as we were praying, I felt the Lord say that it was a prophetic sign that He had come to cleanse the land and cleanse the people. Also, while we were praying, goats and sheep were coming into the church to get out of the rain. And my friend had heard from the Lord earlier in the day that these people had fallen asleep, that at one time they had known about God and had even sought after Him but had since fallen asleep. As we started singing during our intercession, I was led to Psalm 68 and was amazed to see that it confirmed the rain, the praise, the sheep finding a dwelling place, the people being weary…

We were so overjoyed that He confirmed His Word to us, and we knew He would show up in power that night! After everyone left and we pitched our tents, we noticed the large man sleeping on the dirt in the back of the church. He had never left the church! I gently covered him with one of my kapalana wrap skirts, and we all went to bed. At 2:30 a.m., we heard this choking, vomiting, and screaming, and the strangest noises I have ever heard come out of a human being; they were coming from the large man.

Two of our Sudanese pastors and my friend Jennie and I got up immediately, and as we stood over him, we began to rebuke the demons that were tormenting this man. We also prayed in the spirit while the pastors continued casting out demons. We were not timid. We were very forceful and used our authority in that place. The man soon quieted and fell back asleep. When we left this village in the morning, the man still seemed to have a few dark spots in him, but we knew the Holy Spirit was doing a work in him. He got up and left on his own, looking like he was seeing perfectly fine. We felt that he was healed of blindness but couldn't verify it. We stopped at a cattle camp on the way out and said good-bye to the men there and the boys and blessed them. They were very happy we stopped. On the way down the road, we had to part the sea of thousands of cattle that were being herded south in the middle of the road. What an amazing journey we had. Wow!

I later learned that this large man was completely healed of every infirmity and had his vision fully restored. And because he was so drastically changed and set free, the village chief called a service and all were saved and alcohol was banned from their village. They were still alcohol free a year later as we have heard from one of the local pastors. Jesus came like the rain and cleansed this place and these people just as He promised in Psalm 68. His power came as light and rescued those who were walking in a great darkness. He loves every single person on the face of the earth, and as long as there are those who will receive Him, the people will see a great light! Thus began my journey into the interior of Sudan.

After my short-term mission trip with Iris Sudan had ended, I received a very clear word from the Lord to accept a position with another ministry in Sudan. I refused at first because I could not believe that God would do that, because my heart was to be at Iris. Still, I heard clearly from the Lord, and even though I was a bit reluctant, I gave Him my yes for the next year. Six months into that year, the Lord revealed the purpose for this move, and I was so amazingly set up by God. He put me in perfect position for the next season of my walk with Him. I could never have done it on my own. In that year, I had grown more in my spiritual walk than at any other time in my Christian walk. It was an amazing journey and as you read on, I pray that the Lord will reveal Himself to you in a personal way through my stories, struggles, and triumphs and that most of all you will understand what His love looks like on any given day.

joy in a hard place

Living in Africa presents many struggles for both the local people and the humanitarian and Christian aid workers who come to live here. I think that the biggest need in most parts of Africa is clean drinking water. The water in most parts of Africa is not drinkable for those of us who come from the west. It contains parasites that would make us sick while the Africans can, for the most part, remain somewhat healthy as their system has built up a strong immunity to many of the bacteria found in the water. Unfortunately there are more people than not who don't have access to a borehole and must get their water from contaminated rivers and streams and stagnant ponds. This is where many cholera outbreaks occur and many people spend their lives fighting one sickness or another due to an unstable and clean source of water.

The simple things in life that I take for granted are paramount to these here in Africa. I always have to remember how precious water is to those living out in the villages. They travel daily to the nearest town or watering hole and fill many jugs and haul them back in a passing truck, if they are lucky enough to catch a ride. Otherwise, the women carry them on their heads or the men transport them on bicycles over miles of dirt roads or trails.

During the dry season water is even more scarce. My Sudanese friend has to leave her five-gallon jug (jerry can) in a line with about fifty others each day at the local bore hole, which is just a trickle during the dry season, and go back at one in the morning to fill it up and carry it home on her head. Never again will I complain about carrying my jerry can one hundred yards. The dry season also brings vast amounts of dirt and dust because there are no paved roads, just dirt. Whenever I went for a run, I always had grit in my teeth. Even driving my motorcycle, if I didn't wear glasses or goggles, I had so much dirt in my eyes that I sometimes had to pull over and wait until the dust cloud passed. Every time a truck went by, a cloud of dust came with it.

I used to watch the women carrying water and I wondered at how hard it really was. I have always been in great shape, exercising every day, being in the military and such, and I wanted to try and carry a jerry can full of water on my head. One evening I tried it. I thought I was pretty strong, but I was nothing compared to these women! They put a five gallon jug of water on their heads, balancing it hands free, and they walked like a model. I did it, holding on with two hands, and sloshed water all over me, sloshing and wobbling as I walked. Then I couldn't get the thing off of my head by myself and had to get help. One man had a very good laugh watching me I am sure, and finally came to my rescue. It was pretty funny. All of these experiences did give me a greater appreciation for the women of Africa and the daily toil that is a constant part of their lives.

Along with the shortage of clean drinking water in Mozambique and Sudan, the people also lack good medical care. Many of the children walk around with large open wounds and cuts, especially on their feet as they go about barefoot. In America, these same children would be rushed to the clinic or hospital for stitches in a very sterile environment. Here in Africa, the wound remains for weeks or even longer, or we missionaries clean and bandage the wound and pray over it and move on. I managed a child's wound one time after I learned that she had had an open wound on her leg for almost three years! It involved twice-a-day dressing changes for a month, but she is now wound free.

Many of the bush people rely on the local witchdoctor to heal their sick. The witchdoctor uses herbs and local remedies to fix the problem. There is also a sinister element to their healing practice. They put strange things in amulets, such as animal parts and rotten plant parts, for the patient to wear around their necks, telling them that if they take it off they could die. The witchdoctors will even put curses on people to keep them sick so that they will have to keep coming back and pay more money. It is a never-ending cycle. This really does happen. When our teams went to the bush to bring the good news of Jesus Christ, we would always tell them that the power of God is always stronger than the power of the witchdoctor. I go into greater detail on this subject in the chapter of this book about healing and miracles.

I regularly visited a few hospitals in both Mozambique and Sudan and found the conditions to be the same in both places. At one of the hospitals I visited, there were three very large tents on the front lawn, which was nothing more than dirt actually. The hospital was remodeling a wing, so the patients had to move into these tents. They were not very sanitary and people came and went all day long, tracking in dust and dirt. There were also many openings for flies and mosquitoes to gain access. All around, there were families sitting in groups on the hospital grounds with their family cook-pots and dishes, camping there for the duration. This is very common all over Africa. If a person is hospitalized, the family is required to provide food or they go hungry.

We went inside one of the wings. The rooms were large but packed full of beds, some right up next to each other, next to complete strangers. The aisles were only wide enough for one person. Most beds didn't even have sheets or pillowcases. The women had to use their kapalana's (wrap skirts) for sheets. On one of our visits when we went to pray for the sick I had to crawl across an empty bed to get to the person in another bed, the room was that cramped!

There were plates and cups on the floor and on bedside tables, with food and dead flies, and I rarely saw any doctors or nurses checking vitals. People were everywhere, and it was so noisy. Anyone could come in and visit and be as loud as they felt they needed to be. During one of my visits, I was praying for a young lady who had a small baby curled up next to her breast, feeding there in that unsanitary and unhealthy environment. It was obvious the mother was in pain from an eye problem, possibly a tumor on the brain, we were told. Her baby had to live there on that bed and be cared for by the mother as the mother lay there sick. In the bed next to her a lady needed to urinate, and the family was visiting. So one of the visiting women grabbed a bedpan, held up a skirt wrap while everyone continued to visit, and the sick lady had to take care of her business right there in the midst of everyone.

There is a major shortage of medical supplies in these countries, and the hospitals have to make due with what they have. Casting, for the most part, is a piece of cardboard box shaped into a square around the foot or leg or arm, and wrapped with a flimsy piece of gauze bandage or piece of material. Many times people are operated on or limbs cut off without any anesthesia. The only pain pills in these countries are the equivalent to Ibuprofen or Acetametaphin.

I felt so helpless sometimes, and God reminded me that He is never helpless. He is a Father to the helpless, and He is there with them, especially when we come to pour His love out on them and bring a small measure of joy to those places. So many times we would see instant healing when we came to pray for the sick. God just waits for us to go and be His hands, and He does the rest. As I left that particular hospital, tears were falling from my eyes because of the human condition there in that place, and my heart was being opened and exposed, seeing through the eyes of Jesus and how much He loved these people. I did return to that hospital many times over the course of the three months

I was there to hand out bread, juice, and formula and to bring a small measure of joy and love and healing from Jesus.

Sometimes we would find ourselves in the most wonderful situations even in the midst of all this suffering. On one occasion we went into a maternity room, and there were two ladies who had just delivered their babies five hours earlier. One lady was fully dressed and sitting up as if she were a visitor! The other lady was sitting on the floor eating fish and rice out of a pan as if she didn't just have a baby five hours ago! The lady on the bed, I asked her the name of her baby. She said it didn't have a name yet, and would I like to give it one! It is not unusual in many parts of Africa for the local people to ask a westerner to name their child. I think that they feel like we carry extra blessing because we seem to have much wealth. Having even $100 is wealthy in a third world country. When this lady asked me to name her baby, I immediately heard Emmanuel, God with us, and she said it was a girl. I then said Emmanuela, and she could call her Emma. She said she liked that very much, and so it was Emma!

As I continue to live here in Africa, many times I find myself just watching the daily lives of these precious people unfold before me. I step back for a small window of time, and it is almost like watching a movie, very surreal, like watching from a distance, even though I was right there. I went to the market many times with our cook, who also happens to be my friend. I would just watch life as it unfolded around me. There were small fires in various places in the streets for burning trash, which is normal here. I noticed a toddler on the fringes of the crowded street. He was unattended and wearing a dirty shirt and no pants or shoes. He was poking a stick into a smoldering fire. One slip of his tiny, shoeless foot, and he would be in the fire. He couldn't have been older than two years old.

The children are not coddled and hovered over concerning the things of daily life, such as fire pits and cooking knives and planting tools. Many times I have seen small toddlers playing with a twelve-inch butcher knife, as if it were a toy. I have seen them play with small tin cans with sharp edges. The young also learn how to carry hot coals from one fire pit to another. The mothers keep an eye on them but do not interfere with these small ones as they experiment and experience the things that mold the very lives of the culture to which they belong. The children learn at a very young age how to "do life."

My eyes were then drawn to a lady with a baby strapped to her back, a toddler on her left hip, a bucket of something on her head, and carrying a bag in her right hand. I would have had a hard time just handling two babies, much less bags and buckets on my head and such. I also saw a little girl, about six years old, walking behind her mom learning to carry a large, plastic basin of greens on her head, following her mom to market. I watched the brick makers make their bricks one-by-one. They used a wooden mold and squatted down low and filled them with earth and gravel and hay and water and laid them out in long rows, one-by-one, all day in the sun. It's amazing how many they make. This is life in the Sudan. All of this really made me think about how different our lives are, the third world compared to those in a modern society.

On one of my regular routes into the city of Aweil, Sudan, right before I entered the city, I always passed by a field I called squatters field. It is a public field with no trees or tall grass used for growing rice during the rainy season. During the dry season ladies and children use it as a latrine area, squatting for a *long call* (poop), hence the name, Squatter's Field. There were so many sights that became normal to me that, after a while, I didn't give them a second thought anymore. Many times a week I had to drive over a river where grown men and women bathed naked in full view of everyone. Men would stop and urinate wherever they happened to be, although, thank God, facing away from public view. Even on our compound, the local men would face the back fence and take care of business. The women just go to their knees and hike their dress a little and, well, you get the picture. This was acceptable protocol, in Sudan at least.

In the market, I saw the same tired ladies each time I went, either hung over from the night's drinking or worn thin from hunger and the weariness of their lives, begging for money. They were wrinkled and withered and old looking. I would venture to guess them to be in their thirties or forties, yet they looked sixty. I offered them bread or a piece of fruit, and some, those who wanted alcohol, waved it away. They just wanted the money for another drink, which I never gave them. One lady looked at me in frustration and even anger as her baby literally hung like a limp ragdoll on her hip, head lolled back in exhaustion from being carted around all day and night in this heat. I saw her every day this way. I had to almost force her to give her baby the juice I just bought for it. My heart broke, and I felt helpless. I wanted to grab the lady and shake some sense into her, to awaken her from her alcohol induced brain stupor, and take the baby and run and cradle it to my breast in protection from its own mother. I wanted so much to save these children.

Sometimes I look at things here, and it just doesn't make sense. How can a people so oppressed and so persecuted, for the most part, have so much love and joy in their lives? How can a people who have so little have so much peace in their lives? I look at the hard reality of their lives, and it just doesn't make sense how they can be so happy. As I grew to know the people and the culture I learned the reason for their joy and peace. Theirs is a culture built around relationships. Everything they did revolved around relationship, whether at work or at home. I felt almost as if their were no strangers in an entire community. Everyone knew everyone else, and it was very rare to see two people standing or sitting near each other and not be engaged in almost intimate conversation. The people even helped each other to plant and harvest entire fields of crops. It was so wonderful to constantly live in this relational family type atmosphere.

carolyn figlioli

As I traveled around the northern parts of South Sudan I drank in the beauty of the countryside. I took my eyes off of the poverty and sadness, and I looked around at the beauty of God's great creation. It was so green and beautiful in every part of the country during the rainy season. Most tukels (mud huts) had a new springtime roof of fresh intricately thatched grass and everywhere people were cultivating their land, and there was beautiful, fresh-turned earth against a new green backdrop. Adding even more flavor to the scenery, there were ladies in the fields everywhere in their various colorful wraps cultivating the earth. Here in Sudan, cultivating is a family affair. They use long poles with a tiny four-inch-hoe on the end, and they work an entire field on their knees. This type of cultivating varied vastly from the extreme south of South Sudan where they use large hoes and remain in a standing position. The children who were old enough to maneuver a pole were also there on their knees, or standing if from the extreme south, with mom and dad tilling the ground and planting seed. The babies walked or sat in the midst of all the activity, playing in the fresh turned earth and walking behind the adults as the seeds were sown one-by-one. Every day, all day long, they worked, inch by inch. Again, I admired their tenacity, but even more so their relational culture of doing everything together.

Most of the people further north in Bahr El Ghazal grow only for their families, and this is how they get their food for the year. A bad crop or a lazy farmer could literally mean life or death. I found it most amazing that they never refused to help where help was needed. If a family member or friend came to ask for help, it is against their culture to refuse. They simply never refuse, even at the cost of sharing their own meager provisions. When the refugees came from the north after South Sudan became a nation, many villages gave all that they had to feed the starving masses. Families depleted their own rations to feed those who came hungry. The people of Sudan never turn away a person in need. That's relationship. It is the Acts 4 church that God is looking to see across the earth. Everyone shares everything.

Many times I was challenged by the faith of these people. The pastor of one church I preached at told me about his congregation being baptized. My mind was thinking, *where do they go and get baptized, because there is no water around for literally miles and miles except a borehole.*

He told me that the entire congregation walks to the Akuem River, which is at least seven miles away. All the people, the old men and women, the children, the blind even (he said the blind even) walk the miles to be baptized and to witness their brothers and sisters being baptized. These people then turn around and walk back! They traveled about fifteen miles in a day, walking in the heat, singing and praising God, just to get in the river and baptize the newly saved in the name of Jesus! When these people give their lives to the Lord, it is never going to be forgotten, because they have gone to such great lengths to be washed in the river and in His love.

Even many of the church congregants walked from forty-five minutes to one hour away through the bush trails and then back home again to get to and from church every Sunday. The day that I preached the roof was half gone because it was being repaired, so there was a gaping hole where the sun blazed down, yet they still came. Would we show up to church if half our roof was gone, or would we find another church? Hard question, hmm?

The daily lives and struggles of the peoples of Sudan, and many places in Africa, are near and dear to my heart. The longer I live here, the more they become mine and I have learned to cast all my cares upon the Lord. I have found myself in so many situations that would cause most people from the west to throw in the towel and go home. Sometimes I myself was tempted to do the same. I couldn't do this. I was called to Sudan, and I had learned to live here in the peace, the true peace from God, that really does pass all understanding.

Before I joined the Iris team, I served with another ministry and lived in Akuem on a compound. The time was drawing near for Sudan to hold elections to vote for separation from the north. I had sent a prayer request out to my friends in the USA because one of our drivers in Rumbek was held at gunpoint by the Sudanese People's Liberation Army (SPLA) and he was forced to drive for eight hours shuttling guns for the SPLA. The Army was staging weapons for what might come. Our driver was unharmed but it was just another eye opener of how tense things were. Not long after that, we pulled all of our guys out of the region of Rumbek and brought them to Akuem. We also sent all of our Sudanese workers to their home villages to vote. We remained few in number at this distant outpost near the border of North Sudan. Still, I remained at peace knowing that God was with us in all of this.

I was not allowed to leave the compound during the elections, two full weeks, as it was assumed that things would become tense. I was at peace and felt no fear. I believed that God had a wonderful plan for Sudan. There were many in His Sudanese church body who were fasting and praying around the clock for these times and for peace. God would not be mocked, and He would respond to His people. I love these people, and I love their stamina in the face of such trials and their extreme trust in God in the face of the storms that so constantly come. These people teach me what faith is and what perseverance is. They just don't know what the word *quit* means. They smile and laugh and live in such amazing joy through all of this. They have true joy in Jesus. I am learning so much from them. There is so much more concerning the tapestry of the daily struggles and lives of these precious people of Sudan. As we journey on through my story, I pray you will come to know and understand them more and love them as I do.

can a child teach me?

In the Gospels, in Matthew 11 and in Luke 10, Jesus praised His Father in heaven because His Father hid the secrets of the kingdom from the wise and learned and revealed them to the little children. Most of what I learned in my first year in Africa, I learned through watching little children. I learned from the orphans about the Father's heart and the spirit of adoption. I learned from the children's prayers how to really believe in the prayer of faith. I learned by watching the little children how to be content in all things. During my second visit to Mozambique I left with a team on a journey to the village of Namanhumbie in the province of Cabo Delgado. This area had a long history of violence as the hub of ruby smugglers who came from as far away as Somalia and Thailand to seek their fortune in gemstones, because this area was rich in ruby deposits. Children are sold for less than ten dollars. Sex slaves are pregnant at eleven years of age. Murders are a regular occurrence. We arrived in this village late in the evening, after dark, on the Fourth of July. I remember looking up at the night sky and thinking about the fireworks in America and how blessed I was to be gazing upon the beauty of the heavens, unaware of the dangers of being in that place. As I wrote this book, three years later, it had just occurred to me that we arrived there on Independence Day. I think that it was definitely a prophetic sign of what was to come.

When we arrived we danced and sang and enjoyed spending time with the village pastor's family. We were waiting to hear from the village chief about whether we could show the Jesus film that night. Word came back that we could not. We decided to have a worship and healing service that very night in the small straw hut church with no walls.

Some of our team members heard from the Lord to set up a night watch, so we set up a prayer watch throughout the night where a couple of people would be praying in shifts all through the night for breakthrough for this village. The next morning after breakfast, the team began to tell of what they heard from the Lord. Most of them said that the children would be the keys to the village. We anointed each and every child with oil and laid hands on them and spoke destiny over their lives as we ministered to the children for almost two hours. We then went hut to hut to pray for people.

The children led the way and took us to all the places we needed to go. We never went to a single place unless the children said to go there. The first place the children took my team was to the house of a man who could not walk. He said that he used to walk and work just fine, and in the last two years, he became crippled. I asked about his symptoms because it sounded like multiple sclerosis. He described these symptoms exactly. We laid hands on him and prayed, and then we told him to just believe and to rise up and walk. He had not walked in almost two years. He took hold of my hands and rose up and began to walk! As we led him, he walked around the perimeter of his entire yard. His brother was awestruck! Jesus had just touched this man and healed him right then and there in his own yard. We rejoiced together and told them to come to the revival service that night to testify.

We left there and continued on and met a man in the street. He was obviously drunk and wanted to show us his homemade guitar. He sat down and was almost falling over because he was so drunk. The children were laughing at him because they knew him as the village drunk. I reached out and put my hands on his head, and we began to rebuke the spirit of alcoholism. Soon this man was lifting his hands in the air, and he gently lay back in the dirt. He wasn't falling over drunk, he was overtaken by the Holy Spirit! I said, "Let's baptize him with the water from our water bottle!" Now technically, according to the Gospels, someone should repent and then agree to their own baptism because it is a conscious decision to lay down your old life and commit to the new life you have in Christ Jesus. But I felt such a strong urging to do this, and so I just did. After we poured some water on his head and baptized him, he sat up and was sober, completely sober!

We couldn't understand his language, so we took him to the pastor who confirmed that he was the village drunk and was now sober. This man told the pastor that he had been waiting all his life to meet this Jesus, and that his name, Joe Pinaca, means "When I will meet you." Amazing how God picks our names! He denounced his former life and said he wanted to follow Jesus who had completely set him free in the dirt. Joe continued to hang around all weekend with us, because he was so hungry for more!

We left Joe at the church and went in search of more souls who needed to know the love of the Father. The children took us to a house where a lady had been locked inside a hut for five years. We were told that she had been taken to a witch doctor because she was going crazy and becoming violent. Her family took her, and the witch doctor did something to cause her to be in a trancelike state for the next five years. The family had locked her in this hut, which was a chicken house. When we entered the hut, she was lying on a cot in the fetal position. There was a foul odor in the hut, yet the hut looked clean. I felt like I could actually taste the evil that was in there, it was that strong.

There were three of us, so we sat around her and just began praying and declaring the blood of Jesus over her. Then we started to sing over her, love songs from the Lord. After a short while, we felt like we should get her out of that hut. The whole time she would not look at us or even acknowledge that we were there. There was such deep darkness in her eyes; you could tell that something evil resided there. We gently lifted her up and walked her outside.

The mother and sister said that she had not walked or been outside since being put in the hut five years ago. We sat her on a chair and continued to sing over her. Soon word spread and many came to watch us. The witch doctor also came. She began speaking curses at us, but we continued to sing. At one point, the witch doctor was an arms-reach away from me, literally sitting next to me. I looked the witch doctor in the eyes and I told her that Jesus loved her in her own language. She gave me a hard look and shook her head no. I gently told her again that He did, and she just looked at me, no anger, no malice, just a quizzical look.

After about two hours of being with the demon possessed woman, more of our team came and joined in the fight for her life. Soon this woman began looking around at us. Soon tears began to fall from her eyes. She was coming to life, and the tears kept falling because of the overwhelming love of God for her. It was so amazing to watch the transformation in her eyes and face. We loved her and clothed her and fed her while the family looked on in shame at what they had done. Then the mother and sister gently took her to the bathing shelter to bathe her, washing away years of dead skin. We all gathered around them and prayed for reconciliation for this family and release from the bondage of the witchdoctor even as the witchdoctor looked on.

While all this was going on, the pastors on our team learned that a small square hut right next to us was built to house this woman's demons; there were so many! The family had to actually spend what little money they had to feed these demons daily or they would die, they were told by the witchdoctor. This is how deceived and afraid the people are of witchdoctors. Witchdoctors are a very real threat against non-believers in Jesus Christ. The pastors asked the family for permission to tear the house down. We believed that this woman could not be completely set free until this house of evil came down. The family wanted to talk about it because they feared repercussions from the witchdoctor, who was still there. The pastors talked with the family and explained the power of Jesus and His blood. I think because they saw the miracle already taking place with their daughter that they relented and gave us permission. We were told to come back at 6:00 a.m.

The next morning, we were there, and the woman was now living with her family and not in that hut. She still hadn't spoken or shown any emotion except for the tears, but she was now very aware and awake in her spirit. We built a fire outside the compound fence, and the village people were there in numbers. The men tore down and burned the roof while we prayed in the Spirit. Then the men began to demolish the clay walls of the hut. Soon the men were standing on the rubble and singing worship and praise to God. Elisa, the precious lady who had not spoken or shown any emotion in five years, looked at these pastors, and a big smile came upon her face! It was beautiful. Tears came down my face, because I had seen this woman set free. Then the men began preaching salvation from on top of the rubble, and the entire family got saved!

> The people who walked in darkness have seen a great Light; those who dwelt in the land of intense darkness and the shadow of death, upon them has the Light shined.
>
> Isaiah 9:2

The next morning before church, we prayed for a lady whose daughter was deaf and mute. She had never spoken or heard a sound in her ten years. I had prayed for her the night before during our revival service, but it was so loud next to the speakers where we were hemmed in, I asked the lady to come in the morning first thing, and we would pray for her. The team prayed, and within minutes the little girl's ears were opened and her tongue was loosed! I knew then that God had delayed the healing because we were in front of that loud speaker the previous night, and it would have shocked this little girl's ears as it would be the first sound she would hear. She had to learn to form words, so she would just try to mimic sounds. The mother was so overjoyed that she gave her life to the Lord.

The previous day, we were also able to witness to a seventeen-year-old boy who received salvation. One of our team members then spent the next few hours discipling him. By the time we began to pray for the sick at the revival service, she encouraged the boy to join with us and lay hands on the sick, and they would be healed. He did, and they were! Here was this new Christian, only a few hours old, and he was already walking in the power of God! His friends, who had been making fun of him earlier, were now rushing to him to receive the same. The kingdom of heaven came down upon this village in such a powerful way, and I believe that it was because we followed the children and blessed the children and taught them. We left that place rejoicing in the mercy and kindness of the Lord and how He had impressed upon us how important it was to listen to the children of that village. They were the eyes and ears of the village. They showed us the treasures that were hidden, those we could never have found on our own.

Living at the Iris Yei Children's Village, I learn new stories almost every day about the lives of these little ones and where they have come from and every day I learn from them. There was a baby boy at the Center who seemed to be about two years old. He never walked, and when you held him, he tensed his legs so tightly against you that you couldn't put him down. He never said a word, and he stayed so tense all the time, except when his brother held him. His brother was about twelve years old and always held him and loved him.

He chose to care for and feed his little brother over play. Only when the "mama," who also cared for him, held him did the older brother go and play; but he always came back to care for his baby brother again. I learned that this baby was wrapped against his mother's back when she was hacked to death with a machete by the LRA. He witnessed the brutal killing of his mother while he was on her back. This story is all too common in this place of war and violence. God is healing this land and these people as the harvesters come. I am drawn to these people. When I pray for them, I literally weep for them. I have never wept so much for a people. They are so humble and beautiful, and God loves them so much. This young boy's dedication to his baby brother taught me about commitment and perseverance and trust. A twelve-year-old boy taught me this by his actions of love and nurturing toward his baby brother.

I am also so impressed with the servant hearts of most of the people in Sudan. Whenever a guest came to visit the Children's Center, every single meal was presented on a tray, and chairs were placed under a tree, and water was brought to wash the hands of those who came. The girls even prayed over the food on their knees! I am humbled and touched to the core by their servant hearts. In everything they did, this character never changed. Even young boys and girls of eight years old or so washed the babies every night and cared for them while the mamas took care of other chores. They all helped to do the laundry and bring the food to feed the littlest ones and scooped food with their fingers to feed the smaller babies who couldn't yet feed themselves. I prayed fervently that I too could carry this spirit of humility and servanthood away with me more than any other thing. I have learned so much from these children about the kingdom of God. I wanted to see more of the character of God and I knew that I would as I continued to live and learn from the children of Sudan.

I am always meditating upon Isaiah 60 because it was spoken on the day I was born in synagogues all over the world. I feel a special connection to this scripture. Someone once described the glory as this: When you go to a jeweler and want to see a beautiful diamond, he takes it from the display case where it has already caught your eye, and he lays it upon a black velvet cloth. This black cloth brings out the brightness even more in this precious stone.

I meditate on this and think about how, when we go to the darkest of places, we are that much brighter against the darkness there. When we carry Jesus in us, when we truly carry His presence, when we are set against the darkness of this world, we are a precious and beautiful gem, full of the glory of the Lord, and this light and brightness should cause people to stop and look. I wonder, *Is anyone looking at me today? Is anyone seeing Christ in me, the hope of Glory?* I wonder why there is a diamond called the Hope Diamond. The children cause me to think of these diamonds. The children catch my eye and I see Jesus in them, His light.

Sudan has not known peace in fifty years. Just since 2006 are they even tasting a little of it, and there was still so much corruption. The children here have grown up running from tanks, bombs, and land mines. They have been afraid to sleep at night, for fear they wouldn't wake up. They have been afraid to walk to school, for fear they would never see their parents alive again at the end of the day. They have been afraid to walk on the smaller trails, for fear they would be abducted or killed by the LRA. They have been afraid of coming home only to find their family dead and mutilated. They have been afraid to be at a church service, because this was the first place the LRA would go. Many of these children have only known violence. Children are strapped to the back of a mother as the father or an LRA soldier machetes her to death. Other children are beaten daily because their parents have never known anything but violence. This is a country that has grown up in fear. And yet...

One Sunday after church, at the Children's Center, there were five teenage girls visiting together. The girls brought out chairs for their two friends to sit on. They brought out a nice small table to set the tea and bread on that they offered to their friends. After a bit, the girls then brought a plate of lunch to their friends, offering it to them on their knees with their heads bowed in respect. Yes, they really presented it on their knees in the dirt, because I was there, and I noticed the dirt on their knees as they got up. They brought a pitcher of water to rinse the hands of their friends before the meal and watched their friends eat before they even got their own lunch. They waited until their friends were done and had had plenty before they got their own. This is the culture of Sudan! This is the culture where the children grew up in total violence.

When I watched this display of true humility, I saw the woman with the alabaster jar at the feet of Jesus and Him telling the owner of the house, "You didn't wash my feet or my hands when I came in like she has done. You didn't offer me a kiss when I arrived like she did." These children who have been so abused by their own parents and other people, just like Mary, they loved so deeply and honored others above themselves. I am so humbled by them; so humbled. Love understands and love honors others.

> Do you see this woman? When I came into your house, you gave Me no water for My feet, but she has wet My feet with her tears and wiped them with her hair. You gave Me no kiss, but she from the moment I came in has not ceased to kiss My feet.
>
> Luke 7:44-45

One day I was watching as young children were throwing rocks up into a very tall mango tree, trying to knock down some mangos that were about thirty feet up. Earlier that day, they were practically fighting over these small golf ball sized mangos that weren't even ripe. They weren't having any luck, and I joined in the effort and threw sticks and rocks, but nothing was coming down. We saw a single mango hanging low enough to almost reach with a long bamboo pole we had. It was still just out of reach, until I climbed onto a jagged tree stump and was able to knock it down.

They then picked it up and offered it to me, the only mango. I could not take it. I wanted them to have it. They refused and kept holding it out to me like an offering. I was the guest here and deserved the mango, even though I could easily have purchased fifty mangos. I took two bites and insisted I was full. They finally accepted it and shared it among themselves. Then some of the children were able to climb the tree and brought down about ten nice mangos; although still small. They came running up to me and gave me the largest one. This was the Sudanese culture that I had been experiencing. This was love and honoring others, *always* giving their best to another before taking for themselves.

Would I give my biggest mango if given the opportunity? Or would I pick out a nice one, reserving the best for myself? I wanted to learn how to give my biggest and best mango, even giving it to someone who could easily purchase a truck full. I wanted to learn to kneel in the dirt and give an offering of love and honor to another, regardless of who they were and how well I knew them. What I do for the least of these, I do for You.

> And the King will reply to them, Truly I tell you, in so far as you did it for one of the least of these, you did it for Me.
>
> Matthew 25:40

I see how the Father loves us, and I experienced this love every day as the children ran up to me outside our compound gates in Akuem, always calling my name, "Kalowina! Kalowina!" They said my name over and over again from far across the field of dirt as they ran to me, one little boy always naked and in flip flops. When I went for a jog, they ran after me and ran the entire way. They never left me alone.

The little boy, naked and in flip flops, ran the entire one and a half miles with me, and he didn't stop. He was only four years old at the most! I had never seen kids like these who ate just lentils and rice and ran the way they did. One afternoon after running, I just picked this little boy up and hugged him so tight and told him over and over how amazing he was. He didn't understand a word I said, but I think he knew that I thought he was amazing.

As I was editing this book I learned that this little boy died, and my heart grieved so. I am making a special dedication to my smallest of friends, Chiet. Every single day without fail, he stood at the front gate naked as the day he was born and called my name whenever he got a glimpse of me, excitedly hopping from one foot to the other. I always stopped what I was doing and went to the gate to lift him high in the air and hug and kiss him till he laughed. Whenever I went for a run, he would run with me, wearing only flip flops, if that. One time he had a cold and couldn't stay up with me and the other children, and he started crying. I stopped, turned back, and hoisted him on my back, and we ran on.

Chiet went home to be with Jesus. I just saw Chiet two weeks before this, and he was healthy as an ox. I was told that he had "a lung problem," which could have been pneumonia or malaria. I was so extremely sad, and I cried and cried. I felt so helpless. I thought, "If only I had been there, I could have prayed and paid the money for his hospital tests and care." If only's get us nowhere. They just bring more pain.

I honor Chiet's life by saying how much he taught me about love and never giving up and what it must be like to love someone so much that you would run naked with them on the hot sand, even when you were sick. Chiet loved me more than that. This is how our Papa God wants us to run after Him, fully abandoned, without shame. Chiet, we will run again, my little prince, we will run again. Ana hibu ita culu culu (I love you fully always)!

The children were like little magnets. Sometimes I had to tell them to stay and wait for me as I come back around on my run course, because it was so hot for them, otherwise they would follow me all the way. There was a little boy who hung out on our compound and he found me no matter how hard I tried to hide. In the morning when I snuck away to hide and get quiet with God, he found me. He always found me. He loved me and wanted to be with me. He slept on the floor in my office near my feet on a small mat for his nap. He didn't want to go anywhere else. He walked back and forth in front of my office door always looking in, just to get a glimpse of me.

The children outside the fence, they knew where my tent was, and when I went for my shower. They literally waited there to see me coming and kept calling my name through the fence, over and over and over. One morning, they were peering through the fence, waiting for me to wake up as I slept in for once. I have to smile and remind myself that this is how we should love God. This is how it should be with us and Him. We should wait outside the fence near His tent, and when we see Him coming, call His name over and over and over.

God is showing me through the children how it is with Him and us. He says, come to Me as these little children. Run after Me calling My name from across the expanse that is between us. Come after Me naked in your adoration and unashamed in your flip flops. Come find Me, and I will be found by you, even when it seems as if I am hiding, I will be found by you. Come take your rest at My feet. Come walk back and forth in front of My dwelling place until you catch My eye.

Another time, after returning from R&R, as we drove up to the compound, the children were coming from all around to greet me. It was crazy. I would go into the market place and hear my name, Kalowina, everywhere. It made me smile, because the kids were the best part about being there. They were so happy and friendly and never got tired of coming to see me.

One day I went to a village soccer field to deliver a long awaited soccer ball to a small scruffy team of young boys. They had heard that I was bringing them one. I have passed out many since being here, and the kids normally scream, yell, grab the ball, and run off and play, and my existence is forgotten. When I came up to this small group of boys, they came as a team, quietly, and stood before me, quietly, and actually talked with me.

They handed me a sheet of paper that had their entire team roster on it, neatly printed, handwritten, and the name of their team, which was called God's Children United from Al Ha Tarakia Village. After visiting with me for a short time they took the ball and went about having a very organized practice led by a slightly older boy. These boys were only about eight years old. I was so amazed watching them work together on plays, older boys helping the younger ones. This was how the world should be. Can we learn from little children? Yes, we can. I do every day.

Recently, as the school semester drew to a close, I heard children coming down the road singing. I jumped up and ran outside to investigate and to watch this procession of school children, all ages, singing and clapping, coming down the dusty road. I asked what they were doing, and I was told that the children were singing and escorting their teachers home. They do this at the end of every term. I jumped up and ran outside three different times that day, because it was so fantastic and joyous to watch them go by. I was so inspired by how much these children honored their teachers. Can we learn from little children? Yes, we can. I learn from them every day. I learned about honoring others above myself. I learned about honoring my Teacher. I learned about running after my Father, unashamed and full of joy. I prayed that the world would learn this way, from the actions of the least of these.

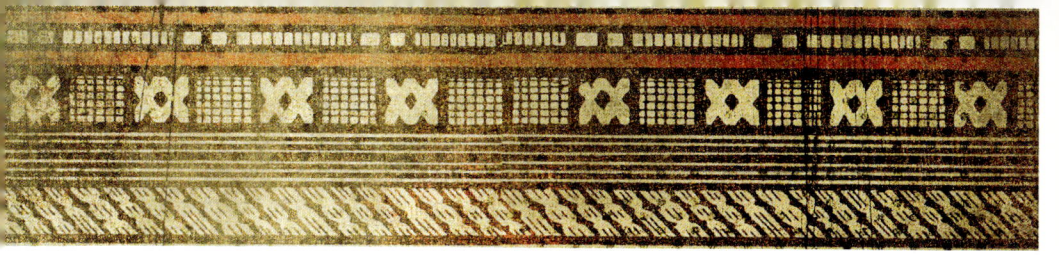

photographs

Bush Outreach in Mozambique Village (2009)

The Blind Man Sees (Mozambique, 2009)

Fresh Bread (Pemba, Mozambique, 2009)

Mundari Women (South Sudan, 2009)

Mundari Mother and Child (South Sudan, 2009)

Mundari Women (South Sudan, 2009)

Mundari Men with Faces Painted in Mud
to Attract Single Women (South Sudan, 2009)

Mundari Single Women (South Sudan, 2009)

Mundari Cattle Camp (South Sudan, 2009)

Mundari Cattle Camp (South Sudan, 2009)

Mundari Cattle Camp (South Sudan, 2009)

Mundari Man and Brother Moving Cattle
to New Water Source (South Sudan, 2009)

Local Village Children (Yei, Sudan, 2010)

Dinka Villagers from Rumbek, South Sudan (2010)

Akuem Dinka Children (South Sudan, 2010)

My Home in Akuem, South Sudan (2010)

The Boy with the New Shoes in the
Aweil Market (South Sudan, 2010)

A Dinka Tukel (Akuem, South Sudan, 2010)

An Early-Morning Forage for Cooking Wood
(Akuem, South Sudan, 2010)

Preaching at the SPLA Third Battallion Barracks Church (2010)

My Jogging Crew (Akuem, South Sudan, 2010)

The Local Water Hole (Akuem, South Sudan, 2010)

Girl on a Village Path Carrying Firewood
(Akuem, South Sudan, 2010)

Young Dinka Boy Showing Me the Way
(Akuem, South Sudan, 2010)

At the Lasu Congo Refugee Camp, Five Miles
from Congo Border (South Sudan, 2010)

Myself and Some of the Congo Refugee Children
at Lasu Refugee Camp (South Sudan, 2010)

My Daily Walk with the Orphans
in Yei Children's Village (South Sudan, 2010)

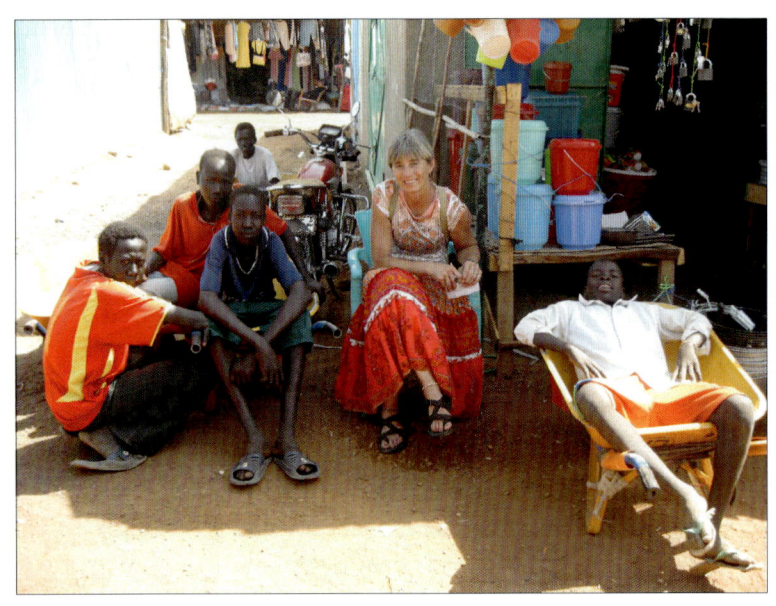

At the Aweil, South Sudan, Market,
with the Wheelbarrow Goods Transport Boys (2010)

Bush Village Children in Mozambique (2009)

Three of the Children from
Yei Children's Village and Myself (2011)

going north

In the spring of 2010 I moved to the small community of Akuem, Sudan, which is near Aweil on the map, just below Southern Darfur. Akuem is up in Dinka Tribe land. It is a village with one small market. The Dinka are one of the tribes who have continuous wars over cattle, and we were close to the northern borderlands. I felt such an excitement about going north, never realizing that God would break my heart for this region. The temperature in March was 120-130 degrees, and there were few trees, scrub brush trees really, with no leaves, and lots of dirt and flat lands. I would be living in a tent, safari style tenting, and I was told that there were three to four inch long scorpions crawling around at night. The tents being safari-style canvas tents, about ten foot by ten foot and seven foot high, were set up on a concrete pad, supposedly to keep the scorpions out. Hmm…

I can't explain the peace that I felt, except that it was God who was doing this in me, it was His grace, that took me step-by-step to a higher level of faith in Him than I had ever known. I was going to a place where there were no other western women anywhere. I would have only Jesus to lean on when the going got rough, and it would. Although I didn't welcome this part of the move, no women about, I wanted to know what that kind of dependence on Him looked like.

When I arrived in Akuem I didn't even know how to say hello! It was an entirely different language. The people were speaking to us in Arabic proper when I had somewhat tried to learn Juba Arabic up to that point. And they spoke Dinka most of the time. I was in for some major language education.

As our plane took off from Yei at seven o'clock on a Thursday morning, the weather a cool, dewy seventy degrees, my mind was already in the north, excited about the new tribe I would finally get to meet and my new home up north.

It wasn't long before the terrain began to change to dirt and scrub brush as far as you could see. Everything was flat and dirt made up most of the terrain. As we landed in Malualkon, where the airstrip is for Akuem, many local Dinka came out to greet us. Many of the children were dirty and covered in a layer of dust that made them appear almost white. Boys of maybe seven or eight years old were walking around naked. I rode in the back of our Land Cruiser to our base about a half hour away to get a better feel for the sights and sounds. The fencing there looked like big woven palm frond floor mats, and they were hung side-by-side to make compound fences.

We arrived at our compound, and the first thing I noticed was that there wasn't a single piece of grass on it, not even a blade, not one. There were a few scruffy trees scattered about, but not many. All of our cooking was done over a charcoal fire, on the ground, the pots resting on some bricks. We boiled water for drinking or bought bottled water. I went through eight to ten twenty ounce bottles a day for weeks, and I just couldn't get enough.

The beds were made of either flimsy metal frames or tree limb type wooden frames with twine strung in a woven fashion as a box spring. The frames were only about six feet long, which amused me because the Dinka are the tallest people in the world! Since I had a "Bug Hut" tent, which is basically a mosquito net in the shape of a tent, I slept inside this on the floor of my tent. The tent that I lived in for six months had a broken zipper on the front door, so the flaps remained open day and night. These were to be my living conditions for the next six months.

That first night, just before dark, I went for a walk around the outside of the compound with two of the local ladies. We stopped and talked to some ladies at the borehole and as we were leaving, there was a snake coiled on the path. I jumped back and realized it was dead. The boys at the water hole started laughing and the ladies too. They placed it there on purpose to scare us, and we all had a good laugh. They accepted us into their community because we took it all good-naturedly.

By 9:30 p.m. that first night, I was still guzzling water and wondered how on earth I would manage to stay hydrated. We were told that the weather had been quite cool the last few days (about ninety to one hundred). Ha! I actually got sunburned from going back and forth doing things to clean my office and move into my tent. I also learned that if there was any way to fit in quick with the local women, it was to do what every woman and girl in Africa do every day, go to the borehole and pump water. So, every evening I would meet the ladies at the borehole to pump water and I tried to learn some of the language. They laughed at my comical attempts to learn their language and I just laughed with them and kept pumping water. I think they liked the fact that I never felt offended when they laughed and just laughed with them and that I kept showing up every day to learn more.

I guess I should describe a borehole. It is a hole drilled very deep in the earth, maybe fifty to one hundred feet down, until it hits a vein. The water that comes out is almost pure. There is still dirt because there are no water pipes or filtration. So, when it is boiled and cooled, all the dirt settles at the bottom. There is also a thin layer of slime on the top that we strain or skim off. It actually tastes perfect after all this, and the color is just slightly off. I am serious when I say that water had never tasted so good in my entire life. If you have ever wanted to give to a water drilling project in Africa, it is so badly needed. I can't imagine working in the fields or outside anywhere. It was just so hot and water is so vital here.

That first week I drove to Aweil, which is south of us, and I went price checking and bargaining. The drive in was so eye opening. I had to drive through cattle herds and over bridges, big steel ones, and there were really small villages right next to the bridges and rivers. At these shanty town type villages, the huts were only made of woven mat walls and roofs. A hard rain seemed like it would topple the entire thing, but they remained sturdy and standing.

We ate lunch at an Arabic place that was so delicious. We ate with our fingers and dipped big pieces of round pita-looking bread into meat and sauces and such. And they had this really sweet, white, thin milk mixture to drink that was so good. It is called Tamarind fruit. Out on the street again, I stood there just taking it all in. There were various groups of men sitting in the shade smoking from water pipes with long flexible hoses, which is just flavored tobacco filtered through water. Across the street there was a mule hooked to a cart being loaded with huge bags of rice. There was an old, old man asleep in his chair under a shady mango tree while the dusty street was bustling with activity.

There were men everywhere with the Arabic attire of long, white, shirt dresses over pajama type trousers. Aweil is very close to the Arabic Muslim north and their cultural influence was evident in the area. The women wore skirts and blouses or one piece wraps with another multicolored one draped around it. Not many women covered their heads, so the Muslim influence was minimal concerning the more strict laws of the north. While we were in the market looking at things, I walked in to one stall and interrupted a Muslim man in his prayers. He just got up and rolled up his mat and so nicely helped me. I kept apologizing for interrupting his prayers. He was very nice. As we were waiting for our guys to get their tools and such, he offered my friend and I a chair to sit on while we waited.

We sat there chatting with these boys who moved empty wheelbarrows around the market to help people carry their purchases, kind of like shopping baskets, but you had to pay them to help you. As we were chatting with them, a Muslim man from the stall across the way came and offered us afternoon tea for free. This was just their way of being hospitable. It was the most amazing place, Aweil. I loved it there, simply loved it. The further into the north I traveled, the more I loved the food and the people. I kept saying that I felt like I was in an Indiana Jones movie, and it was so true. My eyes and my senses just kept drinking it all in; it was so amazing.

I was talking with some of the young men there who are Dinka. One of them, his father has eleven wives, and his mother is the sixth wife. It is Dinka law that the oldest son, no matter what wife he is from, must get married first. And most Dinka do not get married until they have many cows to offer in marriage. The men I was talking to were waiting for their turn in their respective families for marriage, and they were already close to thirty years old. If you wanted a good wife, you might pay up to two hundred and fifty cows easily. Until a man has obtained that many cows, he doesn't marry, or he marries at a lower standard.

I asked them if the Dinka believe in purity until marriage. He said that it is Dinka law to wait and not have relations until marriage. If it is found that they have had relations, the girl's father may force the marriage and ask his price concerning cows. The boy's family must pay, many times paying on credit in the terms of owing the cattle, or a war ensues, and honor is lost for that family. So, sex before marriage brings much dishonor and even war in this community. Again and again I was so impressed with how much honor means to these people and how much it is ingrained into their culture to be hospitable and respectful. It is very disrespectful to just walk into someone's house or office and get right to the business at hand. You must ask how they are, how the family is, tell them they are welcome, and shake their hand

and offer them water or tea if you have it. It takes so long to get things done here. Even our visit to the market, which would have taken easily two hours in America, took all day.

During my second week in Akuem, I was hit by a bacterial invasion that literally took me to my knees for days. The first day I was so sick, and it was one of the hottest days yet, I literally laid down on the hard, concrete floor of the office, which was just a concrete building with a corrugated tin roof, so you can imagine that it was still not a very cool place to rest, and I slept there all day in the corner. My tent was like a slow cooker during the day, so I couldn't even think of resting there.

I had to trek across very hot sand to use the latrine so many times that I wore a fine trail in the dirt with my melting sandals as the sun beat down on my tired body. By the third day I still hadn't eaten a bite of any food. We decided that we got some very bad meat in the local market. The cows were butchered in unsanitary places and the meat was then set on planks of wood day after day in the busy market with dust and flies covering everything. There is no electricity in the village markets, therefore no refrigeration.

I looked back on the almost two weeks that I had already been there, and because of our extreme living conditions I had been unable to do any effective ministry. I cannot begin to describe to you the constant heat. It chases you down, and no matter where you go, it finds you. We had no refrigeration, so there was not even a cool cup of water to relieve the constant thirst. I won't even begin to talk about no such thing as air conditioning. All night long my sheets were wet from my sweat. Sometimes I just got up and stood outside to cool off before crawling back into my sauna for another round. Most times there wasn't even a breeze. It was miserable.

There was so much filth and trash there in that small town. Many times I went into the market in Akuem, which is just half a mile down the road from our compound, and I was overwhelmed the entire time by the stench and the trash that was everywhere. In Yei Town, at least trash was gathered in a pile in the street and burned. There was nothing that I could see there to resemble that. There were plastic bottles and bags, food wrappers, animal dung, you name it, scattered all over the place, caught up on bushes, littering yards and all over the fields. When I returned from walking in the market and changed my dress, my dress smelled just like the market, it was that strong.

Even on our compound there were hypodermic needles still being found in the dirt. It was a TB testing base at one time, and when they left, they just dumped it all over the ground, and there it remained. When we took the base over, we were able to clean most of it up. Still, every day I would stop to pick up exposed needles to throw them away so we didn't accidentally step on them. All around the back fence there were still uncountable needles lying everywhere.

Also on our compound, the latrines were built years ago so there were years of human waste in them, and the place where they put our tents was right where the two latrines were, so there was always this waste odor hanging in the air. Everywhere I went in the market I smelled this human waste smell. People would just squat and go wherever they wanted basically. On one of my forays into the market I stopped at one stall and asked what they were selling, and it was cow manure for fire chips. They had these little cans with little round, candy-sized balls of it too. An old lady came up, bought a round dung ball, and just popped it into her mouth as pretty as you please! I almost lost it!

I have since learned that in many of the cattle camps, the people stand behind cows as they pee and hold their head under the flow to ward off mosquitoes. No kidding! And it is not unusual for locals to leave their meat set for five days, unrefrigerated, before cooking it to eat.

The flies here drive you crazy. They never, ever stop hounding you. Even at 5:00 a.m. they were there in my tent attacking my face. The only escape I had was in my bug hut net, but it was even hotter in there because air can't pass through easily. When I had to visit the latrine at night, I had to set my headlamp at the top of the doorframe or my face would get attacked by these huge latrine flies that were vicious. When you finished your business, you had to be quick about leaving, because they would literally chase you out of the latrine as you went.

One morning I had to go into town early to the meat market. It is an hour drive into Aweil, which is a cleaner city. We decided not to buy our meat in Akuem anymore because of the filthiness of the market and the meat stand. I was still sick and not eating very much, my stomach recoiling at the thought of food six days later. I stood in the meat market in the early morning hours watching whole cow heads, fur still intact, blood dripping out, being wheel barrowed into the meat market. Cow legs with hooves intact were also in the bottom of the barrow. Needless to say, I did not eat lunch again that day.

I feel like I and the people of the western world have been so clueless to this type of existence or we have just chosen to ignore it. It is such a pitiful place for these children to try to grow up, yet they seemed happy nonetheless. More than half of all Sudanese children die due to unsanitary conditions and health issues related to sanitation. Day after day I saw small babies digging through piles of trash and small children running around unattended. These children were barely able to walk, yet they wandered the paths alone. As I grew to know and understand the people and culture, I knew that they cherished their children and loved them just as much as any other part of the world. This was just their way.

I continued to visit the women at the borehole most every night. Even while I was sick and had very little energy, I would make an appearance to greet them and pump a jerrycan or two of water with them. The old ladies were so extremely friendly and would cross a field to come and shake your hand and say hello and even kiss your hand. They were so loving. The younger women were a little more reserved but never failed to wave and smile hello. Walking through the market, it was normal to have a trail of children following you, constantly calling out, "kawaja."

There is so much need in this part of the country that if I looked at the whole picture, I would have felt so overwhelmed. The 2011 statistics from Save The Children show that there are 4.2 million children in South Sudan, 51 percent of the population. One in nine children die before their fifth birthday and one in seven women die during or immediately after childbirth. Twenty-two percent of South Sudan's children are acutely malnourished. One in ten children complete primary school, where there are three times as many boys as girls and the drop out rate for girls is the highest in the world. God always reminded me to start with love, and the rest would fall into place. The Dinka are a very proud people and very resistant to change of any kind. I wanted to find a way to instill cleanliness and sanitation into their daily lives and I wanted to communicate with them and learn their language.

Throughout that week of sickness and heat stress and the daily struggle of just living there, I had also been getting a deeper understanding of the reality of God being the only plan. Living in a third world country, there is literally no plan B. Without God, I die, with Him there is life, always. I was learning what true perseverance meant and what He was saying to Paul when He told him, "My grace is sufficient." That week I thought, "Oh God what am I doing in this seemingly God-forsaken place? How will I ever do this?" I even dreamt that I saw an angry, dark cloud in the sky, and it was in the shape of Satan's face. In my dream I looked at it and said, "Satan hates Sudan." The conditions were so horrid and so inhumane sometimes that I knew Satan surely hated that place. But I also knew that God loved Sudan, and He would never forsake her.

I prayed that I would persevere even under the harsh conditions. I prayed to stay in the fight and to stay strong, to not listen to my flesh when it screamed at the injustice of its treatment. I prayed to live from the heavenly place where Jesus was and would always be with me. I prayed to be moved by what was moving Him in Akuem. And I prayed for the unity of my team because many were quitting. It was a very hard place to be, and we needed each other to be in agreement about our purpose and how much Jesus cared for us. I also prayed for people to always remember and support missionaries all around the world who are far from their homes and loved ones.

One Sunday morning I picked a plot of land on the back corner of our compound near my tent, and I just began to worship God with such abandon. I didn't care who saw me or who heard me. And then I noticed something amazing. In the middle of this large area of dirt stood one green sprout, about eight inches high. It was the only life in at least a forty-square-foot plot. I felt God say to me that there was life in Sudan, a place that had known so much death for so long. The harvest was coming. Get ready and keep sowing. I even took a picture of that tiny sprout because I was so amazed that anything could grow there.

During that difficult time I also had a vision of myself sitting in the middle of a dirt road with my head bowed, my knees pulled to my chest, tired and weak. I was wearing my favorite blue dress with little white flowers. I still have this dress today and will never throw it away because of its significance in my life in Sudan and this vision. In my vision I saw Jesus coming up out of the desert toward me and He squatted down and lifted my chin. Then He took my hands and pulled me up and put my left hand in His strong right hand and said, "Come, let's do this together." I needed to hear those words from Him to encourage me as I continued to live under such harsh conditions. I knew that it would not get any easier, but I also knew that it would all be worth it, so I kept pressing on and pressing into Jesus. This is what His love looks like. He never leaves us in a hard place. He comes to tell us that we can go through it together. We are never alone.

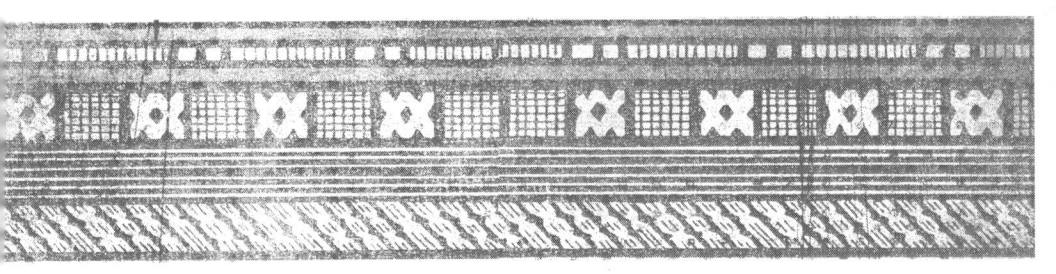

what does love look like today?

Living in a third-world country, I saw poverty and death and dire circumstances every day, and I would constantly look around to see what love looked like to these people. I found that love didn't look the same everyday. I had to look through the eyes of Jesus at each situation, and He would show me what love looked like. Sometimes He would surprise me. Well, many times He would surprise me. On my second visit to Mozambique, I had risen early one morning, as was my custom, and it was still a bit chilly out, in the fifties. At the Iris base there were always guards posted because there was a lot of criminal activity in the city. That one particular morning as I was making my coffee, I thought, our guard must have been cold standing the watch for twelve hours in the dark, and it was in my heart to make him a cup of hot coffee. To make coffee, we boiled water and used instant coffee, and I always checked the boiler kettle to make sure it was empty before I used it because I didn't want parasites in my stomach. I dumped out what little water was left in the kettle. I then measured exactly my cupful as I did every morning, pouring the water into my cup and then into the kettle. Bottled water is precious and costs money, so I always got an exact measure of what I needed. It was while my water was boiling that I thought it would be nice to give the guard a warm cup of coffee also. I decided to make him a cup when mine was done, because I had to measure his in a different cup.

As I poured my water into my cup, I found that I had a whole cup extra in the boiler! Jesus multiplied the water! I couldn't get over it because I knew I had measured perfectly as this was my habit every single morning! My gosh, He cares about all things and all people and wants to do so much for us! I just rejoiced all the way to my morning devotions and smiled so big.

I then went to sit quietly for my morning time with God. I asked God that morning, "I wonder how it is with these children here at the Center, how they see so many people come and go in their lives?" Every week there was another group of visitors. I felt a comfort when I got to know all of the people my first week. I felt like I belonged there. Then, when most had gone home, I felt a sense of loss. Yet these children did this week after week, loving everyone with their whole hearts it seemed.

And then Jesus spoke to my heart. He said, "Do you know why I gave you an extra cup of water this morning? When you think you have nothing more to give, I give you that extra cup of love, that extra cup of grace. I give you more when you think you have given all you can give." I wanted the warmth of that love flowing out of me. I couldn't do that on my own, in my own strength and heart. Jesus poured out grace, and I stepped in. And it took an hour and a half of waiting on Jesus in my quiet time that morning to hear that. I sat there quiet in spirit and what He spoke to me that day came like a slow river, gaining momentum as I went with it, with Him. After that day, I made that guard a cup of coffee every single morning until I left. I have never forgotten where grace comes from and what it looks like. It looked like a hot cup of coffee that day.

I am learning more and more how very important it is to set my affections on Jesus above all else. He has to be the most permanent and important thing in my life. When all else fades away, He remains. I also had to learn to love everyone that passed in and out of my life in the same way that He does, without thinking about loss, only through the eyes of hope. I couldn't do this with my love. It had to be His love, where there is no loss or hurt. Only peace remains with Him. No sadness, just a joy in having known that person for the time I was given with them. I wanted to love like Jesus. I needed Him to help me to discern a balance, so that I didn't grow weary in loving. He was showing me what love looked like.

One morning while I was worshiping the Lord, I kept singing, open the floodgates of heaven, let it rain, let it rain. And I asked God, "What are the floodgates of heaven?" "You are the floodgates of heaven. Open up, and it will rain!" He said. And He caused me to immediately hear Psalm 24,

> Lift up your heads, O you gates, be lifted up, you ancient doors, that the King of Glory may come in! Who is this King of Glory? The Lord strong and mighty!"
>
> Psalm 24:7-8

He reminded me that heaven is in us, and we are the gates; we control the floodgates. We control how much of heaven is released. During the service later that same day, I was holding a little girl and I had my eyes closed and was worshiping God. The worship was in Portuguese, and I didn't understand much of what was being sung, and I didn't really care. God was telling me to always enjoy the day, enjoy where I was whether I could understand or not, to enjoy each day, and watching what He does, I had to open my eyes and really see Him in everything. Immediately after I heard this, I looked around me. To my left stood a little boy about twelve years old, staring at me silently and he had tears running down his face. I was moved with compassion. I reached out to draw him to me and my hand touched his face. He was so hot with fever. He was on fire with fever. My immediate thought was malaria because he was so hot.

I gently put the little girl I was holding down beside me and I placed my hands on the boy and started to pray. After a few minutes, I called a friend over, and we both prayed. I gave the boy my water bottle and had him drink a couple of tiny sips. We continued to pray. After about fifteen minutes, I had a "suddenly" thought. The floodgate word I had received that very morning came to me, and I knew it was for that little boy. I kept my left hand on his head and raised my right hand to the heavens and said, "Lord! Let us be the floodgate and rain love all over this little boy!"

Immediately, the boy started to vomit violently. It was all over the dirt in front of him. It was like a fire hose loosed. All that was in him was expelled. Bamm! The gate burst open. Then we poured the rest of the bottle of water over his head and neck and kept praying. About forty minutes had passed from the time we started, but the fever broke soon after the floodgate word. Praise Jesus, praise Jesus! I was led to continue to pray and I held him for another hour. When I left, the boy was smiling and he looked so much better and felt cool to the touch. Love looked like rain that day.

So many times God would tell me something, give me a word, and it would be about what happened the day before or what I would need for the day to come. Like the word about the floodgates and having to decree that to loose that boy's fever. Or when I made coffee that morning for the guard, and it was the message of grace I would need for the coming days.

As I started each day in the quiet place with God, I would sit and wait. Very rarely would I get there and start talking or praying or worshiping. I would sit and wait and "think on these things." I would ponder things and spin them around in my mind. And then the questions would come and God would speak. It was so easy. I quit looking at troubles and trials as irritations and problems or inconveniences. I started looking at them as ways to see the secrets of the kingdom of heaven. Many times it was through these tests and trials that I grew and was empowered for the next thing.

When I encountered setbacks or problems, I could have looked at them and missed truth. When I stopped to wait with my heart and spirit engaged with God, the answer, the truth, was there. Many times, it was not clear until I actually started walking in the direction of the solution, following the inner prompting of Jesus and Him telling my inner man what to do, even if it didn't make sense or seem to be the right time or the right word to say.

While I was at the Iris Children's Center in Sudan, there was a little girl, about three years old, who wouldn't let anyone hold her. She cried when you picked her up and struggled against being loved. I decided one day as I picked her up that I would hold her until she quieted. She struggled a bit and cried a bit, nothing too loud, and as I tried to soothe her, I remembered how my spiritual mom, Lestra, had sung over me when I was in Mozambique, and yet she was in America praying for me. She sang over me from all those miles away, and I knew I was protected in that song of love over me. My own mother never sang over me, and my spiritual mom's act of love filled the heart of Jesus and filled my heart with such peace when I needed it.

So I started singing softly over this little girl, and little by little her cries turned into whimpers and her whimpers went silent and her muscles relaxed and the peace of the Lord enveloped us together. It was the best feeling when He brought His peace to this little girl. The Lord sings over us. Zephaniah 3:17 tells us that "...He will rejoice over you with singing." If we listen for His voice, we will hear Him singing over us, and we shall have peace. This is the nature of God. He created music, and all creation flows in a harmony that only He can orchestrate. It is up to us to harmonize with Him. My spiritual mom says that we each have our own special song that the Lord sings over us, and I believe it. Love looked like a song that day for this little girl.

Another day I heard this young child just bawling and blubbering and almost screaming on the road beyond our fence. Finally, I could stand it no longer, and I went out to investigate. There she stood in the middle of the road, maybe four or five years old. And I knelt there in the middle of the dirt road and comforted this child. I couldn't speak her language, but love needs no language. It is a language unto itself. I actually made someone wait to handle business with me at my desk, so I could go to this little one. And do you know what? No one objected. How could they? Love must come first. It just must. I wiped away her tears, talked to her soothingly, kissed her forehead, and she went on her way, crying no more. I went back inside to looks of wonder from the compound workers, and smiles. They were not accustomed to someone stopping their work to comfort a child in the street. That is what love looked like that day.

Can we imagine that Jesus will never, ever relent in His pursuit of us? Can we imagine being loved this much? Where He would stop what He is doing and run out into the middle of the road to kneel down and comfort us? What can we say to this? *Nothing* can separate us from this kind of love. Not even a dirt road in the middle of Sudan. He will come to us. Are we really convinced? Death, life, angels, demons, present, future, past, heights, depths… Is there something here that comes between us and the lover of our souls? Only if we allow it.

During the time that I lived in Akuem, Sudan, I went many times to visit the TB/HIV hospital in Wongjok, a thirty minute drive from us, to play with the children there. One day we arrived and all was quiet. You couldn't even tell that children were there. They were just lying and sitting around, not doing much of anything on a beautiful Saturday afternoon. I guess word got out from our last visits and soon the children began to come, even from outside of the fence. We played games with a soccer ball and every child was able to kick and play. Most of the girls in this culture are not able to play ball, because it is considered a boy's sport. The girls spend their days carrying their mother's babies and cooking and carrying water and cleaning clothes. You could see by their faces as they watched that they wanted to play too. So, when we came, the girls got to kick also, and the boys were fine with it. After a bit, we let the boys have their own soccer game where they could go all out while we did crafts with the girls.

That day, there were two little boys who were really sick and they just stood and watched us play. One boy had some really large tumors on each side of his neck, even to the point of severely affecting his voice to where he sounded like a very high-pitched little girl. Another boy was severely malnourished and his arms were just barely bigger around than the neck of a water bottle. We learned that he had TB. Both of them moved very slow and gentle. We encouraged them to join us. Every time it was their turn to kick the ball, you could see their strength begin to increase. I knew that it was because of the joy inside at being able to play and kick a ball. The one with the tumors and bandages all around his neck wasn't even going to come play, because he was so used to just sitting things out. We promised his mother we would be careful.

As she watched her little boy play and saw his joy and strength increase, she too became so happy. Her smile was priceless. After the activities, we brought all the children together, and we praised the soccer players for their agility and strength. We told them about Jesus Christ in them and how He was more powerful even in the weakest of these boys than the strongest man in the world. And we praised the strength and agility of the Lord Jesus Christ in them. We blessed them and prayed over each one, and they were already asking, "When will you return?" Next week of course! We left them smiling and laughing and full of joy, those who were so quiet just two hours earlier. Love looked like a soccer ball that day to two little boys who had forgotten the joy of play.

The Lord reminds me so often that I can't change the whole world, but I can help change a little bit at a time. The problems of the world are enough to overwhelm anybody. I didn't come to Sudan with a grand plan. I just came to help one at a time, one child at a time, one mother at a time, one village at a time. Every little bit helps, and I don't have to be a hero to anyone. I just bring Jesus by way of giving what I can, where I can. He is showing me that love has many faces and looks different to different people. If we would just go and sit with people and listen to them, He will show us what love looks like to that person. He is calling us to go, one person at a time.

One afternoon as I was on my daily jog, I ran past an older woman who was talking to two teenage girls on the side of the road, and they were standing around a very large cooking cauldron. This cauldron was industrial size, big enough for me to sit comfortably inside, cross-legged. It had four handles and was made of steel. I ran by, not taking a lot of notice, and all of a sudden I heard the Lord, "Go back and help that woman." I looked back, and the girls were gone, the woman was sitting on the side of the road mopping her forehead, all alone with this cauldron in the road, leaving me to wonder how those girls disappeared so fast!

So I went back, and she couldn't speak English. With my limited Arabic, I told her I wanted to help her. We set off down the road, down a trail, through the village, down another road, up another trail, and through another village. It was a long way, maybe a mile carrying this heavy steel cauldron. It was so heavy that I had to switch carrying hands about every fifty yards! I can't even begin to wonder how this lady carried this thing on her head! I know she did, because she had one of these round things that they put on their head to carry stuff so it balances better.

These women just amazed me with their quiet strength, never complaining, just doing what needed to get done. She refused my help at first, and I had to insist that I wanted to help her. It was so hard for these women to accept my help, because they were so accustomed to doing for themselves, and not very accustomed to a westerner stopping to help carry a steel pot. At the end of our one mile trek, this woman was so very happy to have had the help, and I left her with hugs and smiles. I re-jogged the path we had just walked and arrived back at the compound satisfied that this woman was home before dark, struggling no longer, at least for today. Love looked like carrying a steel cauldron with a tired woman down a bush path that day. Love looked back when His still small voice whispered.

One of my friends who lives in the village came to work one morning and told me that this lady in the village was crying and sobbing because her baby was swollen all over its body, and she didn't know what to do. She took her baby to the clinic, and nothing was helping. We went to the lady's hut to pray for her baby. She wanted us to also pray over her house, because she said they had experienced so many bad things since living there. I told her I would come back to pray over the house on the weekend as I had to get back to work at the compound.

I saw her a few days later in the marketplace, and the baby was with her looking much better. A few days later I went back to the village to her house and spent some time praying for her and the baby and over the land and the house. She was so grateful.

It is an effort to go and minister many times, especially in South Sudan where it is very hot, the streets dusty and dirty and there were always people wanting things from you as you went. The huts are small and hot, and it would have been so easy to just sit in front of a fan, drinking a bottle of water and enjoying a day off. But when I went to those who were in need, I felt so renewed in body and spirit. It was as if God opened the heavens and rained down on me, and I was filled with life. Love replenishes and fills us up. When we love others, we find that we are renewed in our hearts and encouraged to keep running the race set before us. There are so many opportunities to stop for just one person and show them what love looks like. The opportunities are endless.

One Sunday we went for our weekly trip into Aweil for lunch and we found an ice cream machine! Anything cold is rare to find in Sudan, much less anything frozen! We were excited to say the least. We got a strawberry cone for one Sudanese pound (about forty cents). I took three licks and was thoroughly enjoying myself when my eyes were caught by two small girls and two boys with raggedy clothes, their big eyes watching us savor our ice creams. That's all it took for me. I walked up to the three-year-old and handed her this big, pink cone. Her sister and two brothers looked at her with their eyes popping out, and she just looked at it. The sister and brothers bent in and took quick licks and still this little girl didn't know what to do, but she knew it was hers and was holding on tight. As we walked away I was happy to see that no one had grabbed it away, the children were still leaning in for more quick licks, and still she held on tightly to that cone. I don't know if she ever took a lick, but I think these kids might have tasted ice cream for the first time by their expressions. It was fun to see what love looked like that day for those children. It looked like a strawberry ice cream cone.

We continued strolling through the market, and when we were done and just sitting in the shade drinking cold bottles of water, I saw a young boy about six years of age walk by with this agonizing expression on his face, sweat literally pouring down his face, and his feet were bare and extremely pigeon toed. He stopped opposite us near the wall of a large church and slid down the wall in the dirt, exhausted, and he sat there in the dirt by himself and looked at his toes. I was so moved by his struggle and by his bravery and strength to go about by himself. I bought a fresh bottle of cold water for the both of us and went over and sat down in the dirt against the wall next to him and handed him the water bottle. We just smiled at each other for a minute or so. His face lit up.

I spoke to him in Arabic, and he repeated whatever I said and smiled and drank his water. I looked at his feet and his pinky toes were just a torn mess and bleeding, with flies all over them. I prayed for his feet and kept calling on the name of Jesus softly. Then I took his hand and pointed to his feet and my shoes and off we went. The man in the booth next to where we were told me that the boy was very poor and never had shoes. We tried on the first pair, and he cried because his feet were so raw. We went to another booth and looked and looked. By this time a crowd of about twenty people had surrounded us, either because they obviously knew this boy, or they were curious as to what we were doing. We finally found the perfect pair of shoes and the smile that lit up his face and the way he gave me a thumbs up with his small hands, they were worth every hardship I had ever endured in Sudan. That one moment in time was the biggest look of love for me. I was touched beyond description by that amazing smile.

We walked through that market hand in hand, and this boy could not quit smiling. He kept saying Jesus, Jesus, as we went. Although he did not understand me I told him that Jesus loved him and was with him and hugged him and tucked a Sudanese pound in his pocket. His smile lit up my heart, and for five Sudanese pounds a boy could walk the hot streets of Sudan without ripping the skin off his toes anymore. If this was the only reason I came to Akuem, I would go home knowing that I knew what love looked like. It looked like the smile on his face and the joy in his heart when someone stopped for him. Love looked like new shoes this day.

There was another little boy who spent every day from 7:30 a.m. until 7:00 p.m. at our compound. He wore the same ragged shirt and torn pants every day. His shoes were held together with wire. He loved being with me and followed me everywhere. I went to the market and bought him some new shoes and two new outfits, and when I returned with these gifts, his face shined as bright as the lights on a Christmas tree. He didn't like to bathe at all, just like any other kid in the world, and I told him he would have to bathe before I gave him his new clothes. He helped me carry the wash basin, and when I was going to set it up out back behind a building, he insisted on using the big boy (men's) shower room. Our guard helped him, and when he reappeared, his smile went from ear to ear. After that, each day he wanted me to wash his new clothes and soon he would arrive at our compound each morning and first go wash his face and hands and feet right away.

Sometimes I get frustrated because I can't speak the language. I want so much to talk with people and tell them about Jesus. Jesus reminded me that doing for the least of these is about as loud as you can get when telling people about Him. It doesn't take words to show them Jesus. It just takes time to go and do what is in your heart anyway. People see what is being done, and they see Jesus.

I wanted to go and meet the mother of this small boy who hung around our compound all day and learn his story. I took him by the hand and off we went, across a large expanse of dusty field and down a small bush trail. I was led to this pitiful little structure with plastic tarp walls and a dirt floor and one pot for cooking and an old worn out jerrycan for water. She was so skinny, his mother, and she immediately rolled out a nice sitting mat for me. We sat and talked, with the help of a neighbor boy who spoke English. All the way to her house, other ladies and children would stop me and beg for money or food. This lady never once asked me for a single thing. She just kept touching her boy's new clothes and shoes and telling me, "God bless you."

I learned that her husband had died, and she was all alone caring for her three boys. We visited for just a short while. I went very early the next morning, and I found no one home. I left some food inside her small shelter. As I was walking back, she came with her three boys from the all night prayer service at a nearby church. She was dressed simply, and I saw such beauty in her thin, dark angular face. She is a Christian lady and had a quiet strength about her. We soon became friends and whenever we met, we hugged each other. She was so frail in my embrace. I often wondered if she had prayed for food that day and found that love had dropped by unexpectedly while she was out?

On another of my market visits I encountered this frailest of old ladies. Her hair was falling out, her clothes filthy and ragged, she was leaning on a stick to help her walk along, dragging her feet as if it were her last mile before falling. I was driving a truck and I couldn't stop, because it was a busy intersection. I pulled off to the side quickly to get to her, and I reached into my fresh bread bag and handed her some through the window. People were beeping for me to go, and I just wanted to weep, because she was so precious and frail. She was so tired that she didn't even know I was calling out to her and nearby people had to tell her to look behind her. I left her there with the bread, and she kept walking on, head bowed, eyes distant, my heart breaking. Love broke my heart again and I found myself asking for Jesus to break it even more.

I saw people every day like this. On another day I encountered a man in a wheelchair, just as ragged, no legs, filthy and frail, pushing himself along down the middle of the dusty, busy street. Again, all I could do was give him fresh bread from my truck window and move on or face mob justice for stopping in the road and disrupting people's lives. There are some shop owners that I see in the market stalls who always gave these people food, a biscuit here, a cookie there, a bottle of water. Even they understood what love looked like.

I sometimes wonder if we are entertaining angels every time we stop for the one. I had a *one-a-day* philosophy there in Sudan. I gave fresh bread or a cool bottle of water or a bag of beans to a frail mother or rice or new shoes to a crying boy, whatever God told me was needed for someone each day. I couldn't speak their language yet, but I could speak love. Love looked at the dark man who stood in the middle of the road between Akuem and Aweil.

He stood up there every day, all day. He is mentally challenged, and was always in filthy rags and didn't bathe. He stood there looking up and down the road, all day long! I wondered what he looked for or who. One day I gave him a bottle of juice from my truck window and a smile. He smiled in return. Love looked like a bottle of juice and a package of biscuits on a hot and dusty road and a voice telling him that Jesus knew who he was.

Once I passed by a large group of people on the dirt road who were walking to the city. It was unusual to see such a large group walking together. There were about fifteen of them. There was an old man tied in to a makeshift bamboo type chair on a bicycle and two men were pushing it along. I continued to drive on passing them by in my rush to get to the business of the day. Well, the further I went the more my heart convicted me to turn around and go back. I thought about all the people passing that hurt guy in the Bible and the Samaritan who stopped for him. I had to turn around. I always took someone with me on the road who could speak the language, so my friend found out the story.

The old man was sick and the entire family was taking him to the city hospital, which was a good six hour walk away from where they started. We offered to take him and two others. They climbed aboard, and we were off again. As we went along, I prayed for him out loud. We got to the hospital and dropped them there, and they were so grateful. I told my friend to tell the old man that I prayed for him. The old man thought that I said I wanted to pray for him, and he nicely told my friend that he didn't need me to pray for him because he wasn't a believer. Too late, I already did. Guess it was a God thing

I still saw the dark man on the road every time we went to town. I always stopped to give him a drink or some cookies, and I would say the name of Jesus to him, trying to penetrate the haze that surrounded his brain and the demons within. I finally did learn his story from one of the locals. Seems he killed his pregnant sister and the elders of the village put a curse on him. He had been that way ever since. It was very sad, and I wanted to see him set free from the darkness that lived inside him. I just kept showing him love as we stopped every time and I continued to pray for his deliverance. Once when I stopped, I really looked at him and I felt like crying, because I had been so burdened with his situation. His eyes were just so vacant, and he didn't have any happiness. I looked at him and his condition and prayed as always, and I said, "Jesus deliver him, no one deserves this." And I thought, "Yes, we all deserve this, but because of God's mercy, we are not left like this."

I would sometimes watch life on the streets and I would feel like I had so little to offer these people. There are more children than adults, it seems, and they are mostly tattered and dirty. They beg all the time or try to get me to buy things I don't need. Sometimes I find ways to let them help me load things when I shop, so I can give them a pound (money) without it being a hand out. There are many old looking women either drunk or hung over. The smells in the air are so bad sometimes, like something died and is rotting. People urinate wherever they like. Trash is all over. The horses that pull the carts are horribly abused, and I looked at one that was literally skin and bones; I am waiting for this one to just fall over dead.

If I looked too long at all of this, I would become so sad and grieved in my spirit because of the severe poverty. I have to keep reminding myself to just stop for one, stop for one at a time. Jesus was always stopping for the one, always. The one sheep is more important than the rest. If he is lost and walking blindly, ignoring the blaring horn of warning, Jesus told us to go after that one. So every day I see the sheep and am reminded to keep going after the one.

Recently, as we went into the market to run a few errands, we found a treasure. A little girl about ten years old came and sat next to one of our team members. She was wearing a tattered and dirty red dress, she was dirty and smelled of urine, her teeth were dirty, and she had scars on her chest and face and dirt caked in her unkempt hair. But she had the most beautiful smile. We talked to her in Arabic, and she wouldn't focus on us or look us directly in the eye. We wondered if she could even hear us. The shop owner ladies told us that she was deaf and that her parents died two years ago and she had been living on the streets ever since, digging in trash heaps and sleeping in shop corners in the dirt.

We took her home with us! We didn't know her name so we named her Mercy because love looked like mercy this day. We fed her lunch, bathed her, gave her new clothes and started praying over her. The next two hours were spent in intense prayer and deliverance. When we first brought her home she was moving here and there, and she couldn't sit still or focus on any one thing and never seemed to respond to our voices or seemed to understand us. She was definitely manifesting dark demons. We also thought that maybe she had been sexually abused because of the way she acted toward men that we encountered on the way home.

After the two-hour session of deliverance and prayer and love, she was calm as could be. She understood everything we said to her and she sat quietly and peacefully to eat her dinner. She could hear! We would say, "Aculu (eat)" and she would eat. We would say, "Casalu edan (wash your hands)" and she would wash her hands! At one point, while eating, she closed her eyes and licked her fingers and kept her eyes closed as if savoring all the goodness of that hot meal and clean clothes and a place to call home where she was set free from the agony of the last two years. That peaceful look on her face said everything that needed to be said.

After dinner and hand washing she was led gently to her new bed, her very own bed, with clean sheets and a blanket and mosquito net. She crawled inside and giggled and was so extremely happy to be in that place. She lay her head down and was asleep instantly, and there was peace in her soul, knowing she was home. Love looked like Mercy this day. "And what does the Lord require of you? To act justly and to love mercy and to walk humbly with your God" (Micah 6:8). This is why I am here. We stopped for one that day, just one, and her life was forever changed and she knew the goodness of the Lord and His plans for her life.

I am sure you have noticed by now that I spend a lot of time going to the market. Since we have no electricity or refrigeration, going to the market is almost a daily necessity. Many of my adventures with Jesus took place in the market. I guess one could call it marketplace evangelism. Early one morning I was in the market and I ran into one of our local Sudanese workers. He saw me and told me that his baby was in the hospital and was in very poor condition, he wasn't eating and had a very high fever. I told him, "Let us go, and I will pray for him." So, I left off what I was doing, and we went straight away. When we arrived at their bedside, I laid my hand upon his tiny, curly head, he was only a week old, and upon the mother, and I prayed for increase of appetite and for the mother's milk to be pleasant and nourishing to the baby. I then gave the man some money, because I knew he got paid by the day and was missing three days work to care for his family. He was so grateful, and I left to continue my business in town. The next day, the man said that right after I had prayed for his baby, the baby suckled at his mother's breast and had been eating ever since, and the fever had left him. Yipee God!

That same day I also saw the man in the wheelchair, whom I had seen on numerous occasions before this. He was in the middle of the street and trucks and tuk tuks (motorcycle taxis with a small covered sitting area) were trying to pass by him. I went out to him and I took his hand and held it, and I just stopped my busy world and prayed with him right there in the street. Then I asked him where he wanted to go, that I would push him. His hands and feet and clothes were just filthy and ragged and soiled, and his hands were rough from pushing a wheelchair, which had no tubes in the tires. He just smiled so big and pointed down the road. So off we went, me actually singing over him as I pushed. What a sight to see, this clean kawaja pushing this ragged and filthy shell of a man, me singing and him smiling and even laughing at times.

We were moving along and people were watching and giving the thumbs up as we went. They were amazed I think at this sight. So many were giving thumbs up and saying thank you, because a kawaja took time to care for one of their own. Marco, that's his name, took me down side streets and behind streets, and we finally came to his yard. His family came out to greet us, and his mother hugged me and told me her name was Angelina. I smelled the liquor on her breath, and I stayed and visited awhile and gave them money to buy Marco's chair new tubes. His mother was overjoyed and kept hugging me. His mother got up right away, and off we went to get new tubes! Soon I had this whole entourage with me going to get Marco new tubes. Love surely looked like new tire tubes for weary hands that day.

What a glorious day. It is always so exciting to be where Jesus lives and moves, among all His people everywhere. My favorite days are when I can be with the dirty and torn and broken people and just do what I can to bring a smile, to both them and me. It always makes my heart glad to stop for another. When I was hungry, you fed me. When I was thirsty, you gave me drink. When I was naked, you clothed me. When I was tired, you helped to push me. What you do for the least of these, you do for Me.

I want to always see Jesus in the people I stop for, one at a time. It only took fifteen minutes to go with the man and pray for his baby. It only takes one minute to stop for the dark man each time. It only took thirty minutes of my time to push Marco and visit with his family and get them on their way to get new tubes. That week I spent one hour and stopped for many "ones." It really is so easy, and it fills your heart with such joy when you do. Stop for one this week, just one, and see what God will do in you. Follow Him. Let Jesus show you what love looks like today in your neighborhood, in your school, in your family, in your church, in your city.

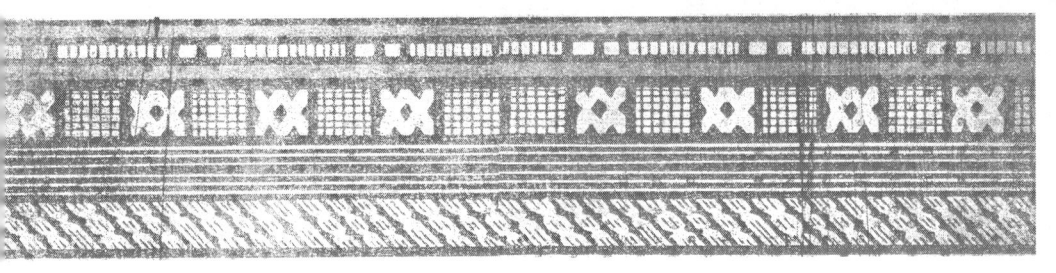

miracles and healing

Every chapter of this book talks about miracles and healing, whether in body or in spirit. I felt though, that I might dedicate a chapter to a few more of the miracles and healings that have left a lasting impression on me and to tell just how amazing God is. If the people are hungry and expecting, God will show up and He will touch them. I think that one of the biggest obstacles to seeing miracles in the west on a regular basis is that we aren't really expecting them. Most people in the west believe God does miracles but not on a regular basis, maybe only for special circumstances. I was guilty myself of this wrong thinking before going to Africa. I could pray and believe for other people but rarely for myself. And I would have this little piece of doubt planted in the rear corner of my mind. What if it didn't work? People would look at me weird. I made it about my reputation and not about what God wanted to do.

Many people want to see God move, but it is usually on our terms. If things get a little weird, like someone being raised from the dead, well, that is just a little out there. I know many people who believe this way in the west. We are actually surprised when it happens, almost as if that wasn't the "normalcy" of God. The people of Africa, they just stand there and expect God to touch them, to raise the dead, to make the blind see, to instantly heal a deep wound, and so on. When I went to Africa, I think I finally got to a place where I wasn't going to fear what I couldn't do but to instead believe in what God could do. If He didn't show up, I wouldn't be made a fool because I didn't know anyone in Africa. God has a great sense of humor concerning me and a lot of grace I am thankful to say. I learned to partner with Him and that took a lot of pressure off of me.

In Mozambique we went to a village called Maricopa. As soon as we arrived, before we even got into prayer, the warfare began. We didn't realize it right away, but one of our team members was stabbed and robbed of his cell phone and shoes while we were in prayer about fifty yards away. We arrived right before dark and had just enough time to set up for the Jesus movie. Some of us played with the kids while the guys were setting up. This village had seen missionaries before, so they knew what was going on. They even had a small established church.

Our team was very large for this trip, so we arrived in three vehicles. While the Jesus movie was playing, the team was praying and worshiping. We were standing and kneeling in the dirt in the dark. After a while, we felt something biting us. At first, I thought it was a sticker that had scraped my shin, so I moved just a few inches. Then I felt biting on my neck, and I knew it was some type of insect. It was pitch dark, and we couldn't see very well, so we turned on the flashlights and realized that poisonous African fire ants were biting us. We were literally stripping off what clothes we could to get them off of us. After we were done shaking out our clothes and brushing ourselves off, we went right back to worshiping, speckled with red welts and itching skin. That probably made the devil mad!

We stayed and prayed for the entire movie, which was about two and a half hours long. Right before the movie ended, Heidi Baker, the director of Iris Ministries, came to the platform and preached. She was fiery and animated. The crowd was captivated. I don't even speak Makua, which was what she was speaking, and I was excited and captivated! This was the Holy Spirit at work in the midst of us. Many received Jesus as Lord and Savior. After she was done, she told the team to split up into twos and threes and pray for the people, for their needs.

All of the prayer requests that we received that night were for headaches and deafness. It was all head stuff. All of the headaches that we prayed for were healed in Jesus' name! There was a young boy, about ten to twelve years old, who was hard of hearing. We prayed and soaked him in Jesus' love for a bit, and then asked if he could hear, sign language of course. He said no. We prayed some more and then asked again. He said no. We prayed some more, and then he excitedly motioned to his ears and shook his head yes. Praise Jesus! His ears were opened.

Then a woman came up who couldn't hear at all. We prayed for her, and I felt led by the Holy Spirit to rub her ear lobes. I felt a little foolish, but I did it anyways. We prayed for a bit and asked her if she could hear. Well, we actually made the motion as if asking her. She said no a couple of times too, and then finally, her ears popped open; she was excited and wide eyed. It was simply amazing! At this time, Heidi had a young girl and a woman up on the platform with her, and they had both been healed of deafness. Wow! What a night! The healing presence of God was felt by so many. We continued to pray for people when all of a sudden, one of the male team members told us, with a bit of urgency, that we needed to get in the truck.

We could feel the tension in the air, but we could not get into fear because that would exalt the enemy. Faith exalts Jesus. We helped to load the truck. Then we were told that the pastor of the village wanted us to bless his little church, and so we walked over to this little church. Many of the villagers followed us. They were very noisy, and I don't know what they were saying, but I didn't think it was a very positive atmosphere. We reached the church and the entire team and some congregants crowded inside this little mud-hut church, shoulder to shoulder practically. Some village people were outside and they were hitting the walls and saying things through the cracks in the walls to distract us. We just praised God and sang and danced and clapped and prayed and had a great time. Dirt and dust and sweat were thick in the air, and we didn't care.

In the midst of it all, I had this vision of looking up through the roof at all the stars and the heavens, declaring God's glory. And I had a glimpse of what the end time church in the book of Revelation was going to be like. In that mud-hut church we had men and women from many nations and many tribes and many tongues, all worshiping Jesus, every tribe and every tongue confessing that Jesus Christ is Lord. I was overwhelmed that God would so bless me to bring me to Africa to this place for such a time as this. Tears of joy rolled down my dirty face as I took in the glory of it all.

And then we all sat down in the dirt, no fire ants were invited, and ate a simple spaghetti noodle dinner with a light tomato sauce. We were served out of one very large community pot, out of their poverty, yet out of their riches. As we left the church and were walking back, a couple of boys ran up and stole a woman's kapalana from her hands and someone's camera. It did not dampen our spirits or ruin the night because Jesus did so much there that night. Even if we only came for one, it would be worth it, fire ants and all. The enemy will always try to steal and destroy. It is our part to keep moving forward with what God is doing. Never let the enemy destroy the good that God has done in a place, even in your heart.

Throughout my time in Africa, I make hospital visits a regular part of my ministry. On one of my trips to the hospital our team prayed for a lady who had just been involved in an automobile accident. Her entire face was swollen and she was in so much pain that she couldn't even sit up comfortably. After we prayed for her there was no visible change but we left with a knowing that God would heal her. The next day when we returned to the hospital we found that this same lady was healed completely and waiting to be released. The day before, she couldn't even sit up because she hurt so much. Now she was sitting up, and there was not a single part of her face swollen. She was smiling and looked really good. We told her that it was God who did such a fast work in her body and was she ready to receive Him as her savior. She said her whole family was Muslim, and it was too hard to answer that question at that time with them standing around her. That is okay, we told her. When the time was right, she would be able to respond to God, because He would keep calling her name.

We also witnessed another miracle at this same hospital, where a baby was healed. A man came up and asked us to pray for his son who had just been born that day. His son's eyes were yellow and were completely covered with a gauze dressing. His liver wasn't doing well at all the man was told. He was a Christian. The nurse would only allow one of us into the room to pray for the baby, so we gathered in the hall and prayed about who the Holy Spirit wanted to go in. I was picked to go in. As soon as I walked in, I knew this baby would be healed because I had seen him in a vision the previous weekend while on outreach to a bush village. As we were worshiping in that village, in a vision I saw a person who had their eyes covered with a cloth or bandage because something was wrong with their eyes. In the vision I started praying one word over and over again in the spirit. I never do that, praying the same word. It was foreign to me, but I felt that God told me that when I see this person, speak that word over them.

I looked for a person with a bandage over their eyes all that weekend while on outreach so I could pray for them, but I never saw anyone with a bandage over their eyes, and so I thought I missed it, maybe I didn't hear God or get a real picture. Then, when I saw this baby in the hospital I instantly knew he was the one I had seen in the vision. I got on my knees beside where the mother was sitting and placed my hand on his tiny head. His eyes were bandaged, and his mom was holding him. I prayed for him and said that word that I had received in my vision over him. And then we left.

When we returned the next day, the baby had been released, fully healed! God healed him! A few weeks later, I ran into the father while I was in town. He said that he was a soldier and that he had spent his day off traveling from his bush village to thank us for praying for his baby. He said it was a miracle about his baby and it was another miracle that we should randomly meet in the street like we did.

On yet another outreach, our team went to three villages in the bush in just over twenty-four hours. We left on a Friday and arrived in time to put up our tents in one village only to drive to another village, some miles away, and set up for the Jesus movie. As I was quietly praying by myself for the people while they watched the Jesus movie, I felt the Lord tell me to ask anyone who was deaf to be brought forward when the time came for prayer ministry. I was so nervous to say this, because I was basically saying God will heal them. So I did it, scared. I asked the people to bring forth the deaf. A young boy was brought up to us by his brother and the team prayed, and within minutes, he could hear because God opened up his ears! He was giving the thumbs up sign and grinning from ear to hearing ear! Praise Jesus! The people were so excited, and many came forward for salvation. What a night! We didn't get back to camp until 1:00 a.m., where we ate dinner, and fell exhausted into our tents at 2:00 a.m.

The next morning we were up at 6:00 a.m., and in the truck with no coffee or breakfast, on our way to do some baptisms. We went to a slimy, stagnant pond under a small bridge and baptized ten people. We sang and rejoiced all the way back to camp, the locals singing louder than any of us Westerners as they were so overcome with rejoicing at the goodness of God. When we got back to camp, we swallowed some rolls and coffee and went to dedicate a church and perform a wedding. This took five hours! We got back to camp and ate, and then packed up our tents and went to the next village and set up our tents and set up for the Jesus movie.

Again, we prayed for the people, and a man was brought forward who could not see and he had a white film over his eyes. I personally waved my hand in front of his face and snapped my fingers and got no response. We prayed for a bit, and I asked if he could see. He said it was getting better, so we stayed with it. We asked again and tested him to see if he could count our fingers. He could see! He then said that when he came there he couldn't see, and now he could see everything! Jesus healed him! The following week, when we went to another village some miles away, this same man had walked for hours to get to where we were just to testify about what the Lord had done for him the week prior.

Another young boy came forward and pointed to his ears signaling that he couldn't hear. We asked his friends what the name of the deaf person was and we would say it right next to his ear to check for a response. None. Then we prayed. And when we whispered his name again, he repeated it! And when we whispered Jesus, he repeated it! Jesus healed him! There were many more healings this night. We couldn't even keep up with God, He was so excited watching His children pray and rejoice in His goodness.

So many times I found myself stepping out of my comfort zone and praying for people that seemed impossible to heal. The more I prayed, the more I saw God move and heal people, and the greater my faith became, not my faith in my ability but my faith in God and what He wanted to do. I was coming to a place where it was no longer about me saying the right prayer for the right amount of time in a quiet perfect place. We mostly found ourselves in the middle of noisy crowds, being jostled and squished and poked. We learned how to partner with God and stand alongside Him and to be a part of what He wanted to do. It was that easy. Still, I had to get over the last hump. Believing for my own healing.

One afternoon, after I had moved to Sudan, I started to feel achy all over my body, and I was really tired. I had been in the country for almost six months with very few days off, and it was catching up with me. I had the chills and body aches and a fever, so I prayed throughout the night, waking up every hour. Two days before this, I had made many trips to the latrine. That morning I was so weak, I felt like I would pass out. I even went for a malaria test because my eyes could not look at the light without hurting and my head was pounding. I just kept praying.

My friend had asked me earlier in the week to come pray over her property and house and to pray with her live-in-babysitter, because there had been tormenting spirits bothering them, and the girl was having dreams and feeling the presence of evil. The people of Africa very much believe that there are evil spirits and that the spirit world is real. They won't play around with this and many times call on a witch doctor to fix the problem. My friend, being a Christian, called me instead. So, on day four of my illness, I fasted, after hearing from the Lord to do this, and I went over to her house. I spent an hour praying over the house and then the girl and doing what God led me to do in that hour. When I was done, the girl said she felt very much at peace and was so glad that I came. As soon as I finished and was headed back to my place, I was in perfect health, all sickness gone!

I was able to eat again for the first time in four days, and my stomach did not hurt. I decided from that point that I was going to look at sickness in a new way. I would look beyond the symptoms and ask the Lord what was really going on. Sickness is the work of the devil, and he is always trying to stop the plans of God. To destroy the works of the devil, I will do the works of God!

Soon after this incident, a crew worker had come in from the field to go to the clinic. He was sweating profusely, and his eyes were so red. He was obviously sick. I prayed for him as I do every other person who goes to clinic. I actually tell them that they will be healed as they go. By the time I finished my work that day, I started to feel really bad. My skin was tingling all over, my ears hurt, and I was warm to the touch. I prayed on and off throughout the night, taking no medication, just praying and sleeping. I had all the symptoms of malaria again. I went to bed very early, layered in clothes and blankets, in Sudan where it is in the 90's and 100's. When I awoke the next morning I felt wonderful; praise God! It was like nothing was ever wrong with me.

Later that day, the man that I had prayed for the previous day came back and told me that when he had come to see me to go to clinic he was feeling so sick and throwing up that the guys in his crew didn't want him coming back from the site by himself, but he had insisted. He told me that the clinic diagnosed him with malaria and gave him meds. He wanted to tell me that as soon as I prayed for him, as he went, all of his symptoms left! I have since learned from two other missionaries that there is a spirit of malaria in Africa, a spirit that imitates the sickness, with all the symptoms, but does not show up on any malaria tests. I truly believe that I have experienced this spirit and that God delivered me from it twice as I prayed for others. Both times I was tested, the results were negative, yet the symptoms were there. God is so dynamic and so intricate and so versatile, who can ever know His ways about a thing?

I have so many stories of personal healing while in Sudan. I have seen God heal me time and time again. I have reached a point in my walk finally where medicine and doctors are not my first inclination when I am sick. I first go to God and I stay there as long as I can or until healing hits me. Sometimes I take medicine, if I have it, to get my mind off of the symptoms while I pray for the restoration of my body, but I try and hold out as long as I can. That's okay. God is not a legalist. He is love. He is love always and forever. Living in a third world country requires a lot more trust and belief in healing from God because there is no plan B, no doctors or hospitals or medications in the bush. He has to show up or the people perish. I like to bring the good news of the Kingdom of heaven and that Christ in us is our hope. My personal testimonies have become my platform of faith to jump off of, freefalling into His grace!

I met a soldier in the Sudanese People's Liberation Army (SPLA) one day and we started talking about God. He liked what he was hearing and he asked me to come and preach at his church. He was an SPLA Army Garrison pastor. I went and I preached, and heaven invaded earth in that place. God so set us up!

These SPLA men were war veterans. They had had a bad reputation during the war, because they abused their power and many were the stories of torture and murder and the burning and pillaging of entire villages. So many horrors were suffered at the hands of the SPLA during those years. That morning I found myself deep in the heart of the battalion headquarters where the families lived with their soldiers. These men are like Paul who became Saul after meeting the Lord on the Damascus Road. They had been turned upside down by the love of Jesus since the war, and they welcomed me with such warmth and humility. The wives of these men had lived through hell, and their faces were etched with the shadows of what they must have gone through.

I came with the message of the resurrection power of Christ in us in Ephesians 1, 2 and 3 and with the message of Romans 8, where we were predestined to be conformed to the likeness of Jesus, by the power *at work in* us, and we are called, each one of us, to do greater works than Jesus because of this. The presence of the Holy Spirit burned in the hearts of the people that day, and I could feel the electricity in the air every time I mentioned His name. Your kingdom come, Father, *on earth as it is in heaven*! I told the people that God predestined heaven to be planted here on earth. If Jesus said to pray this, then let's bring it to pass. Let's bring heaven to earth now. Why wait to go there? We are already seated there! Then I began telling testimonies of all the miracles I had seen in Africa, even at the hands of little children.

I told everyone who needed a miracle to stand up right then. The entire congregation stood, all 417 of them (they take a count each week)! Then I told them that if they believed the Word that was just preached, then they had the power to do miracles *because of* Jesus Christ in them. They didn't need a kawaja to form a healing line. I had them turn to each other and lay hands on each other and pray and declare the name of Jesus over each other.

This was a new thing for them. They did it and people were praying fervently. When we were finished, I asked for testimonies of immediate healings. So many hands shot up that we could not get to them all! It was amazing! The Holy Spirit moved so powerfully and showed the people that it didn't have to be some visiting white person to have a healing line for them to receive their healing. They saw the power at work in themselves! They saw the great love of the Holy Spirit for them and His desire to see them set free! Backs that had been suffering pain for years, healed in Jesus's name! Stomach ulcers, healed in Jesus's name!

I literally jumped up and down, and we all started jumping up and down and clapping and yelling to the heavens and rejoicing at the power that was displayed there that morning! John, the pastor of this church, told the congregation that he related so much to the story I told about Peter and how he was not qualified to do any miracles, because he denied Jesus three times. Yet, Jesus came and asked Peter to take care of His sheep. John said that the SPLA killed so many innocent people and that they were not qualified, yet Jesus came and forgave them and used them for His glory. The first time I ever heard John speak was when he spoke at a another church in the area and he told the congregation how moved he was that they accepted and loved the SPLA brothers, even though just five short years ago the SPLA came in and destroyed their villages and churches and killed and raped their women and children. They were humbled by the love of the

Dinka people and were amazed at how much they forgave and forgot and loved them anyway. This was the true love of Jesus. Could I do the same if some army came in and killed all of my family after raping them and torturing them? Truly I wondered if I could love my enemies as these had done.

At the end of my message that day, a big man in the front row started to shake and tremble and sob and weep loudly. God was doing something in this man and no one stopped Him. We let this man be and tears came down my face, because I had never seen a Dinka man cry before. This man was breaking, and I think Jesus was touching him mightily with love and forgiveness. It was a great morning of healing, both physically and spiritually.

I want you to know that I had no faith in myself. I cannot heal a single person. I never could. One of my biggest prayers has been, "God deliver me from myself and give me faith to have faith." Faith without works is dead. It can do nothing just sitting there. My healing ministry began when I started praying for the sick. I must have prayed for a thousand people before I saw one miracle. I was so desperate to see people healed that I set up a healing booth at a local flea market in Texas where my friend Kevin and I just prayed for people each week. Many times we didn't even get a single customer. Sometimes we saw miracles and sometimes we didn't see a thing happen when we prayed for people. But we kept praying. When Jesus returns will He find faith? Faith and love are what move God. These three things remain, faith, hope and love. That is my ministry every day. I can do no good thing without them.

the lighter side of life in sudan

Life in Sudan is not always a serious affair. I do have fun for the most part and some times crazy things happen. One can always be assured that when venturing into town they will meet up with an adventure, although seemingly serious at first, to be laughed at in retrospect. There are laws that at first don't make sense, but when one thinks about it, well, maybe they do make sense. At least the crime rate in Sudan is far lower than anywhere in the west, well, except for the occasional LRA village raid or militia attack from the north.

I'd like to introduce you to a lighter side of life in Sudan. You can tell you've been in Sudan too long when:

You hear that a container has arrived with a new shipment of used clothes, and you can't wait to get to the market to find a deal! By the way, these containers are full of donations from the west which were hijacked somewhere along the way and are now found for sale in the local markets. I sometimes wondered if I would happen upon an old shirt or skirt in that market that I might have donated two years ago to some mission clothes drive...

You share your devotions in the early morning hours with a huge spider on the wall in the vicinity of your head, and you continue drinking your coffee not giving it too much thought.

It just doesn't feel right brushing your teeth inside anymore, and you feel this pull to stand outside with a cup for that spit/rinse time.

It feels too weird to throw toilet paper in the toilet. You even feel guilty when you accidentally do it. Of course it is even weirder to see a toilet.

You never put your feet on the floor in the dark without first flashing the light on your cell phone to check your flip flops for critters.

A water bottle feels more normal than a cup.

You forget what ice feels like.

You get claustrophobic if you have to take a shower in an enclosed space, like with a real roof.

You wake up throughout the night, because it is too quiet and that's not normal.

You can't remember what carpet feels like.

Sitting in a plastic chair starts to feel comfortable.

You actually notice when there is no smoke smell lingering in the air and miss it.

You can smell and taste the difference between bore hole water, river water, and filtered water, becoming a water connoisseur of sorts.

It doesn't bother you anymore when people find it normal to pick their noses in broad view of everyone else (no kidding) or to do the pinch one nostril and blow out the other as there isn't such a thing as Kleenex here.

It is not second nature to flip a light switch on when it gets dark.

Your headlamp becomes a part of your head when the sun goes down. And that's keeping it light (oh wait, there is no electricity)!

One day, I decided that I would go for a noontime run. I usually run after work in the evening. As I was running along, I came upon a group of schoolgirls in their cute little uniforms, dresses of course, and flip-flops. There were about ten to fifteen of them.

As I ran past I waved at them and to my utter amazement and surprise, they started running with me. Soon, there were thirty to forty girls laughing and running with me and talking all at the same time and trying to hold my hands, all of them, while running!

It was a funny sight to see. They were all elementary school age, and they ran a very long way with me and wouldn't quit. As we came back around to their school, one of the girls looked at me and seriously said, "You give me money." I would have to say it was the craziest running experience I had ever had, and one I wouldn't soon forget.

Many times when I am jogging, people just start to run with me and laugh as they do, I guess making fun of me, I don't know. Even old women do this! It's the craziest thing. Needless to say, it was very distracting trying to run there. It takes an extreme amount of patience and love to stay in shape, because you just have to put up with it all. Quite a few times I found myself jogging down the street with a seventy year old Sudanese woman, jabbering away in a language I didn't understand, and me listening intently, keeping my eyes open for the cattle herd that might appear in the middle of the road around the bend!

Most people in Sudan are very polite and love to greet the kawajas, the white people. There is one small group though who fear the kawaja. The children under the age of about five, many times scream in sheer terror if a kawaja approaches in any way. A Sudanese man once described the first time he saw a white person, and it makes sense why they fear us. He said that he thought it was a Sudanese man with his skin turned inside out, and he wondered how a person could walk around like that and live.

North Sudan is mostly Muslim, so they are under a different set of laws than Southern Sudan, which is predominantly Christian. I have never seen a law book and am no expert on the laws of the land. I can only comment on the encounters and knowledge that I have had with the law, which I have been cautioned to obey. There are some crazy rules concerning breaking the law here. I think I can see why they do it, make crazy laws, because it sure keeps the everyday crime to a real minimum. I can say through personal observation that there is most definitely more crime in the west than anywhere I have been in Sudan.

Here are some tips on driving. It's against the law to wear flip flops or sandals or even shoes that don't have a back strap on them. Well, all of my pretty little shoes are sandals or flip flops, because I wear skirts every single day. When I have to drive somewhere, I put on my classy brown Crocs, and I look "very smart" as they say here in Sudan. If caught wearing improper shoes, you can go to jail or pay a fine.

African men are not allowed to braid their hair for any reason. Braided hair on a man is seen as criminal activity, and they throw you right in jail for braided hair. If a woman is in town and has tight pants on, she can be beaten right there on the street! I just wear skirts to avoid that little mess. And they can be thrown in jail for being promiscuous. Yet there are the night ladies who are allowed to do what they want, because they are serving a purpose, mostly to the local police force or army unit. Huh?

When driving through a roundabout, which is basically a four-way intersection with a tire or jug in the middle of it, if going straight, you must put on your hazard lights while going through the intersection, although there are no lights or stop signs or yield signs. If the traffic police are standing in the area, they will blow a whistle, and you must stop, or they will run after you! Run after me, huh? An offense warrants a ticket or jail, if they feel like it and if they can catch you! Ha! Everything is a jail offense, if they feel like it.

It is against the law to wear sunglasses while driving. If you are driving, and the street police blow a whistle at you and you don't stop, you risk being chased down, thrown in jail, or shot at. So, basically people don't listen to radios while they drive here. Wouldn't want to miss that little whistle because you didn't turn on your hazard lights because you couldn't see the intersection through your sunglasses.

Picture taking is not allowed anywhere in town. If you must take that memorable photo, you'd better be real sneaky. If caught, they just take away your camera. If you are white and someone runs into you with their car or motorbike, it is your fault because you are white, and you have the money. If you are white and someone hits a goat or chicken or duck or any number of animals and you are anywhere in the vicinity, it is your fault because you are white and you have the money. I am being serious here! I have been working real hard on my tan!

All this makes it very hard to be a good Samaritan, because you will be blamed for whatever mishap it was that caused them to need a Samaritan in the first place. The only way we can avoid giving rides to the SPLA or police is by having this sticker on our trucks that show a gun with a lined through circle meaning, No Guns Allowed. Otherwise, don't stop or they will demand to get in. I ride a motorcycle to avoid that situation.

These are just some of the rules that I am aware of here in the very southern part of Sudan, and I try hard to follow them. Up north in Akuem, it is not so harsh. I wouldn't want to find myself in the local jail waiting for my friends to bring me rice and beans every day. Better to just follow the law, regardless of how crazy it may seem.

There was a bridge in Yei that passed over a river, and there were huge holes in the concrete, as it eroded away, and you could see the water below through the holes. It was the scariest thing to drive over. It was also the only way to the airport. The roads and bridges department does a temporary fix by dropping steel plates over the holes. Every so often they gather all the material to do the temporary fix and they don't tell anyone when this will happen. You could be going to drop someone at the airport and come back to find you have to leave your truck at someone's house and walk across to catch a motorcycle taxi on the other side, and then go back and get your vehicle a day or week later.

This actually happened to a friend of mine! Or you could take your Land Cruiser and ford the river somewhere down the way. It is just so crazy. The bridge has since been replaced by a new one, made entirely of steel of course!

The children around here used to yell at me through our fence, "kawaja, kawaja," meaning white person. Now I only hear, "Carolina, Carolina." I have a name! That is a major step forward for a kawaja here. On their way to school, the children yell, "Carolina, how are you?" When I go to visit they run out to the street to greet me. Of course if I keep giving them soccer balls and candy and beads and show them movies on my computer, why wouldn't they come running? No, I think that they are just great kids, and they like having a kawaja as a friend. It's like having the latest in electronic equipment. I am high-tech for them.

We have these spiders here that I really don't like. Of course, I dislike all spiders, but these kind are really creepy. They are extremely flat against the wall and are about one and a half inches in diameter, and they move so fast. It's as if they just slide zippity quick to their next location. When I see them in the latrine, boy do I take care of business quick and with a wary eye, moving very slowly at the same time! Yuck!

I began thinking about how easily we coexist with all these creatures, them not bothering us and us not bothering them. We are aware of each other and give each other space, not infringing upon each other or disturbing each other. Except one morning, I couldn't help giving a baby lizard a drink of water. I was brushing my teeth at the outdoor sink, and it had been really hot here, and I gently tossed a few handfuls of water on the wall where it was. Then he just started licking the wall. Haha! It was amazing. I was watering the lizard.

I went for a walk around the town one day and everyone knows my name, well sort of, "Kawaja, kawaja!" Some things never change. Among the treasures I found along the way were these little frozen Popsicle looking bags of Gin, Gin in the Bag?

I was even offered a little bag by some guys on the street. I told them if I drank one of these they would have to scoop me up out of the dirt. They laughed and went on their merry way.

Every morning I greet the dawn with the incessant heehawing of a multitude of donkeys that roam about. It's like having a bunch of Eeyores walking around. They heehaw loudly, sounding as if they are in tremendous pain, but they are just hungry I imagine. The cows and horses are skin and bones because of the extreme heat and no rain, but the donkeys are fat as ever. I really don't understand it, because they don't get any special food, just the occasional plastic bottle or garbage bag or rain tarp. Hmm, maybe there is something to be said about plastics?

There are also many hawks in this area and they have large talons. There is one who has claimed our compound as his hunting territory, and in the morning when we get our biscuits and tea, he swoops in to try and snatch your biscuit or bread from your hand and even from your very mouth if you are not alert. It happened to me! I was holding my bread and walking along, not paying much attention, and so fast that I literally did not see it until it had already happened, my bread had been snatched and there was a scratch on my finger, which started bleeding where his talon had caught me. Another man was putting bread to his mouth, and the same thing happened, leaving a scratch on his face. I now walk aware, and I protect my bread!

Every single night I am killing a scorpion. I remember that just a year ago, if I saw a scorpion I would run the other way and get someone else to kill it. Even when I first arrived in Akuem, if I saw one, I would throw a brick at it from six feet away so as not to get too close. It didn't take me long to just walk right up with my flip flopped foot and squash it! I hate them. There is one type that you cannot squash with your flip flop. It is called an Imperial Scorpion and these can be as large as seven or eight inches. One crawled out of a mirum pile, which is the rocky sort of dirt we use for leveling the ground and to prevent flooding.

Our driver ran over it with the seven-ton truck, and the thing kept on crawling! Yikes! I think we're going to need a really big flip flop for that one!

Right before the first rain storm hit Akuem, the wind started blowing real hard and things were banging about and I raced to go to the latrine, because I knew I might get stuck in my tent for a while. I ran inside just in time to see a bat fly down into the latrine hole! Now what? I had to go. I really did. So there I was trying to take care of my business while fending off this bat that is flying around down in that hole! I tell you what, my perseverance concerning this tour of duty in Africa almost came to an end that night.

And finally, the big excitement in town today, my friends borrowed my camera to take pictures in the market, which was illegal as I stated earlier, while I went to take care of some business. I came back to pick them up, and it was right at that moment that an SPLA soldier took my camera from my friend and told her to come with him. My other friend came running and said I had to come right away. There we were, two ladies running through the market with dresses and sandals, hair flying, determined and on a mission. We were looking for this man and my friend and running up and down the alleys of the market to try and locate them. Soon there was a small mob forming behind us, as they knew we were looking for this soldier, and on we ran.

I finally spotted him, very tall, in a suit, dark glasses on, cell phone to his ear, looking sort of like the CIA, walking quickly with my friend fearfully trailing after him. I ran up to him and basically blocked his path by standing right in front of him. I said, "Hey, that is my camera. You cannot take it." He looked at me and got real close with this mean look and said he was taking it because we cannot take pictures in the market. I refused to let him pass, and I continued to demand my camera. I could not believe my boldness here. I didn't even think to be scared. I was mad at corruption and mad at the ridiculousness of it all. I then told him that I had a close friend who was very high up in the

SPLA and that if he didn't give me my camera I would call him right then. I really do have this friend. Then I said my friend's name, and the look on this man's face was priceless.

He immediately gave my camera back to me. We were in the middle of the street, about fifty people around us, a mob, and he handed it back. I shook his hand and even thanked him for being so kind. I asked for his name so I could tell my friend how very helpful he was and he looked at me incredulously and walked away and I went on my way with this huge crowd following me. People were amazed and kept touching me and smiling and shaking my hand. I think they too were glad to see someone take a bold stand against corruption.

Two months before, I would never have been this bold, never. Living here and knowing the culture and learning to not back down, to trust God and His stand for righteousness, that made me bold. Even weeks after that incident I would hear people in the market say in passing, "I want my camera back!" I would just laugh! I am known as the kawaja who got her camera back. I am stopped many times with a smile inquiring after my camera. I laugh and go on. I guess I am famous in that town now. So funny!

About two months after arriving in Akuem I was given my Dinka name. It is perfect for me. I am now called Carolina Akat. The word, akat (pronounced ah-cot), means running swiftly. The children all around Akuem know me, because I run around the airstrip and down to their soccer fields. They would see me running and ask me where I was going, and I have learned how to say that I am going running. Ana le akat! They speak fast here too! Of course I am a big hit with the locals, because I am making a good effort to learn the mother tongue. I really do love these people. They are so precious, and I have so much joy being around them. In all the seriousness of life in such dark places, it is amazing how light the hearts of the people remain. I think that they have learned how to laugh at a young age and know that this is a good medicine.

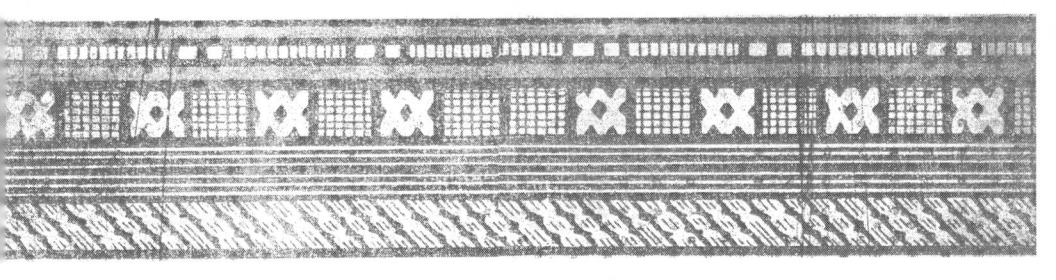

surrender

Mathew 12:39-40 tells us that the only sign we will see of the coming of the end of the age is the sign of the prophet Jonah. There are a number of interpretations of this scripture. I like to think of it the way the Lord revealed it to me for my life in Sudan. The sign of Jonah was that he eventually died to himself. He didn't do what he wanted to do. He did what God *asked* him to do.

Most of us are like Jonah, dragging our heels and running from dying to ourselves. I ran from that process for three years. I would pray, "Oh God, take all of me, do what You want, have Your way," and then I would stop Him if it got too radical. Until Jonah literally died in the belly of the whale, until he did that, he had no power or anointing to do anything. When he died to himself, he carried an anointing to lead an entire nation to repentance and salvation from utter destruction. I wanted to get to that place where I relinquished my hold on this life and let God have His way in me.

The sign of Jonah was not only about resurrection, it was about the death of our identity and our agenda. Jesus is revealing truth to us in these last days that will cause many to turn away. When Jesus revealed the truth about eating His flesh and drinking His blood, many turned away. The disciples knew that there was nowhere else to go. They left everything to follow Him. There was no turning back. They found their identity in Jesus, not in the fact that they were fishermen or tax collectors or schoolteachers or pastors or elders in a church or car salesmen. They had nothing to fall back on except to follow Jesus.

Living in Sudan, I was learning to understand and love this place of being nothing but being found in Jesus, to be where He was. My big prayer was to be of no reputation, to be known only as the one who loves the Lord. At the end of the day my prayer was, "God, help me to finish well, to never weary in doing good." I was always thinking about surrender. In South Sudan, the political climate was getting darker. In the spring of 2010, the people were literally being held captive by the government because they were not allowed to cross the borders for any reason as the vote for secession from the North was going to take place. Up until that time, the people had the freedom to go across the border to visit Uganda and Congo and now found themselves prohibited from going anywhere because the government had mandated that the people stay until the elections in March, and that they must vote.

Just down the road in Lainya County, the minister of one of the government offices was visiting to encourage the people to vote. He was ambushed and shot and was airlifted out. People were caught in the gunfire and killed, innocent women and even children. Four hundred people were camped out in the Lainya Episcopal Cathedral because they were too afraid to go to their homes, because the rebels were still causing terror to further their political agenda.

A friend of mine, a pastor, had just returned from that area, and the LRA were still killing and terrorizing villages and kidnapping young men and women. The youth leader of a church in Ibba was kidnapped, and there were many people being displaced because of their fear of the northern militias, the LRA, or of the tribal violence that constantly spilled over into neighboring villages. And all the while, it was suspected by the people that the northern government was feeding the fires of terrorism by supplying weapons and ammunition to these terror groups. The people were afraid. They left their crops and fields and were facing a severe food shortage because they feared returning to their villages to tend to their crops. Do they surrender to death at the hands of the enemy, or do they surrender to death by starvation? Which is the lesser of two evils?

When you are exactly where God wants you, no matter what is going on around you, you have to learn to stay in a place of true peace in your heart. My friend Viola told me that my heart couldn't contain the hurts that I took in sometimes. I had such a passion for things to be right and good and fair, and when I saw it not so, I took it to heart. It was discouraging to see a situation and feel helpless to do anything about it. The system remained in place, and because you were either a part of the system or on the outside looking in, you had to abide by its rules. I really understood during these times of unrest how Jesus kept breaking the rules and replacing them with mercy. But what could I do when it was not in my power to break the rules of the system?

It made me want to just throw in the towel and go somewhere else where the rules were different. Well, it doesn't matter where you go, the rules might be different, but there will always be an unfair and biased world. So how did I deal with it? No quick answers there. That's what I daily work through with Jesus. Each day presented a new opportunity to practice what I preached, love and long suffering and patience and kindness and all the fruits of the spirit. The cup of suffering is really full of joy unspeakable. I just needed to get my taste buds working.

So, I continued to meditate on surrender. What did it really mean to surrender, to be held captive? And I thought about what I would have done if I were this people who were displaced. What would I have surrendered to? I wondered even, what things captured me, and what did I truly I surrender myself to? Unless I surrendered myself fully to God, then I was wasting my time here in Sudan.

When I said, I surrender all, I wanted to mean it. At that point, I hadn't surrendered all. I continue to work out my salvation until the day of the Lord's coming, as do many of us, and that is all that He asks of us concerning surrender, to continue on in the faith, and to continue on in doing what He has called us to do. I am sure of this one thing: Jesus Christ had to be my peace. I could not even comprehend it, but He really was my peace. I slept like a baby at night. I walked to the latrine in the dark of night, not a care in the world because *I knew* that He truly did care for me. He always looks out for our best interests and He always will. Only in Jesus do I put my confidence. To put it anywhere else, in ministry, in Sudan, in this world, is sheer folly.

On one of my trips back into Sudan after R&R, some of my luggage did not arrive with me. Our office in Nairobi retrieved it for me at the airport. I was told that my remaining luggage would be on the next in country flight in two weeks. I was excited, because it contained things for the children. Two weeks later the plane landed, and I watched every bag unload with great expectation. Then the pilot told me that my luggage made it to the border of Kenya and Sudan, and there it would sit for another two weeks. The plane was carrying too much weight because of extra passengers they took on at the border. I was crestfallen. I had been battling a spirit of discouragement all that week, and then this. Almost immediately I heard the Lord say to me, "Carolyn, if your luggage never came would you still praise Me?" It took me the entire thirty minute ride back to the base to really feel it in my heart, but I said *yes, Lord* and meant it.

I got back to the base and back to work, pressing in to keep a happy face and have a rejoicing heart, and now there were fourteen men staying on our base for the next two weeks. I was the only female and I had to share the shower after them. I had to share the latrines after them. I had to not be offended by their *manly* ways such as blowing snot out of their noses as they walked along, or as they walked around in just a towel after a shower... I was pressing in even more for that happy face and rejoicing heart.

That night, after using the latrine, I found myself cleaning the entire thing at nine at night. Three pastors were watching me do this, hauling water buckets back and forth, and they thanked me when I was done. It was a good feeling. I was working on getting past my *self*.

The next day, our base director asked if I wouldn't mind if his friend, a lady, shared my room for a night. As he left to go get her, I learned that yet another lady was coming. So, I had to move my things under my bed and into a corner to fit another bed from another hut, and then I learned that they were going to be there for the entire weekend, all of this with a two hour notice. And all the while the Lord was gently asking me, "Do you still think that this is *your* stuff, *your* space, *your* hut? Are you really willing to die to yourself?" I had just taught on this the previous week. Then came the test all that week. Could I count even that room that I called my own as loss for the prize of Christ Jesus, of being found only in Him? Could I? By the end of the weekend, I was so blessed because these girls were really sweet, and so nice and we formed a lasting friendship. It was such a blessing to have them there.

Jesus taught me that week that it was not just about being obedient or doing the right thing, but it was about the attitude of the heart. If I had just said yes Lord, but in my heart I still felt a no, then it wasn't really a yes. I had to let Him do His work in my heart all week to get the *yes* of the Lord in there. Only He could change my heart, if I let Him. Since that time I moved twice more to even tighter living conditions and shared the space that was provided. In Akuem I lived in a tent for six months and for over a month I shared that space where there was only two feet between the beds. That was close and comfortable. The Lord had made me ready.

Each week, the Lord showed me how easy it was to really let go of my control of things and let Him show me His ways. His ways really are good. Our God is a happy God, whether we surrender completely or not, He still enjoys us because He created us. On my drive into town early one morning there was a light, misty dew hanging over the landscape. A fog like sheen covered the land, and the sun was just coming up in the east. The ladies were wrapped in vibrant colored material, walking across the dry and dusty land with baskets on their heads, dark and lovely they were. I saw such beauty in the land at that moment, and I drank it in, and I saw the heartbeat of God for His people everywhere and He smiled. I felt the smile of God, and my heart was full of peace. God smiles at us always. He is a loving God, and He never tires of us. He sees our destiny in Him and He never grows hopeless, because His Son came as our hope.

That same afternoon I watched a dust tornado roll across the landscape in front of me as I was returning from children's ministry at the hospital. I had to stop and watch it, because it was so amazing. I turned off the motor, so I could listen to the sound. It was intense as it picked up plastic bottles and trash and swirled and carried away the trash in its whirlwind. It was about twenty-five yards wide and about seventy to eighty yards high. The sound was intense. I thought about God bringing a shaking and sweeping across the land and carrying away the trash and clutter of our lives. When the whirlwind passed, there was no damage to the huts or even the people. God can do this and leave us unharmed. He comes like the wind and we should stand there and let Him strip away the debris, let the intensity of His voice and His wind sweep over us and carry away the debris.

Many people write to me and ask what I need and what can they send. I didn't have much in earthly possessions my first two years in Sudan, but I had what I needed. It didn't make sense, but God was teaching me to be content with less and less. There was nothing that I needed that He didn't give to me. My personal needs had become so small, and the Lord made sure that they were met. Philippians 4:12 describes so perfectly what I felt. "I know what it is to be in need, and I know what it is to have plenty. I have learned the secret of being content in any and every situation..." The Lord really was showing me what it was to be content in all things.

Once, when my iPod broke, I was surprised at my reaction. I just shrugged and said, *what can I do about it?* We tried everything we knew to fix it, and nothing worked. I could do nothing until I went home to the USA six months later for a visit. Why lose my peace? After that, every morning I dragged my computer around, making sure it was charged, so I could listen to worship music on my headphones. I chose peace.

Someone on our compound accidentally broke my coffee press. It was all I had. How did I react (truly I love my coffee)? I didn't bat an eye or miss a beat. There was a small strainer in the kitchen, so I used that little strainer to strain my coffee, one cup at a time, and I drank a lot more tea, which I really do love. What else could I do? I just made the best out of the situations I found myself in, and I daily counted everything as loss compared to the knowledge of Christ Jesus. I really had grown into the mind-set of counting it all loss.

I had one extra toothbrush that I kept, just in case. The little boy who hung out every day with us on our compound, his teeth were in horrible shape, and he was showing me how his gums were bleeding. The Sudanese use sticks from trees to form a brush, and that is how they cleaned their teeth. It worked great for them. This little boy hadn't quite gotten that concept yet. He watched me brush my teeth one day with curiosity. I went to my tent and brought that brand new brush of mine, a beautiful blue and clear Oral B brush, and his own tube of paste, and I taught him how to brush his teeth.

After that, every single morning he literally ran through the front gate and headed straight for my office where we kept his kit, and he would put his paste on his brush and grab his cup of water and walk around the compound brushing for all to see, his tiny chest puffed out. His smile was so bright every single day when his eyes alit on that brush, because it was his. His gums soon quit bleeding. If anything had happened to my brush, I would have counted it as loss and used a stick if I had to. I did learn later that one could buy a brush in the local market.

I never worried about what I would eat or wear. I usually wore the same four or five sets of clothes. I didn't even own a cup or a plate or fork, and I didn't care, because I was just as content to eat with my hands out of the same dish as my brothers and sisters! I would lie on my bed made of tree limbs and twine as a box-spring, and a piece of four-inch foam as my mattress in my bug hut outside of my tent on a piece of concrete, and I was so filled with the peace and presence of God, because I was not concerned with what I didn't have. My only concern was to seek the kingdom of God, seeking His amazing presence, listening for His very heartbeat for us, because that was my living bread and my cool drink of water, and I was clothed in glory there. That was church!

I truly came to a place of such contentment. I do not write these words as a noble script, showing how pious I could be. I honestly feel these things and live in this place of revelation. When I am in a modern city in Africa or America, sure I enjoy the comforts and luxuries of a modern world. That is the beauty of Paul's scripture, Philippians 4:11-12. He tells the church that he learned how to be content with nothing and also with plenty. Either place was just as wonderful for him, because it was Christ in him who brought this contentment. Jesus Christ was all that mattered. Everything else was just a wonderful bonus or a minor affliction. If Christ was my all in all, then He truly was all that I needed, because in Him my riches were found, my needs were met and filled. He cares that much for us! I found this in my life in Sudan, a place of so little yet so much.

My friend in America asked me once if there was a way to live this way, simply and content, in America, a place that had so much. I think it would be hard, because I think that we have so much in America. We spend ourselves trying to please others more than for ourselves sometimes. In Sudan I was happy wearing the same clothes every day. In America I would be thinking about what others would think about me for wearing the same dress to church every week, or making sure that my shoes matched my outfit. In Sudan I didn't style my hair or even wear makeup and I sure didn't match my clothes! It is in style there to not match and I love it. In America I would be wondering how that would cause others to see me. There is so much that is different. Don't ever feel guilty for what you have. You are blessed to have it. Enjoy it. But don't hold on to your stuff so tightly that you lose sight of what or who is really important. Keep the daily pursuit of Jesus as your focus, and what He wants. Jesus surrendered, even in the face of hardship, for the joy set before Him. We are His joy. I surrender the things that I do because I know that then I will walk in true joy, the joy of knowing Him and how His heart beats for even the least of these. His heart beats for all of us, especially when we surrender to Him.

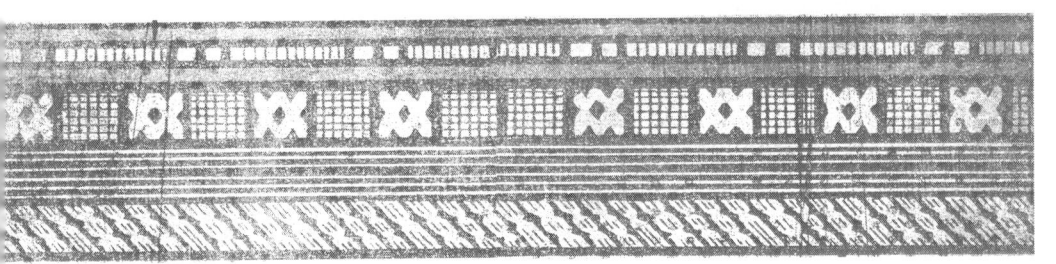

missions 101 will always be about the journey

In the last chapter I talked about surrender and counting all things as loss compared to knowing Christ Jesus. I meant every word of what I said. But I also want to be honest about the times where I felt like giving up because of the harsh living conditions in a third world country and the suffering that went on around me. Sudan is both beautiful and harsh. In the deepest south, the land is rich and green and food is plentiful for the most part, if people are left alone to plant and harvest their crops. The northern part of South Sudan is dry and rugged and desert like, and food is scarce in the harsh summer seasons. I thought about all the things that were hard about being a missionary in a third world country. My spiritual mom told me that I should let people know the difficulties that I faced, that "it ain't easy being me." So, here are a few of the struggles that I had to get through and get past:

I missed my family and friends so much sometimes. At my first base, for almost a year, when the locals went home at the end of the day, there were only three guys and myself left on the compound. I spent most nights in my room or tent by myself. I couldn't go anywhere after dark because it wasn't safe. It was very lonely sometimes.

I missed the comforts of home sometimes. I thought about how I couldn't even get a salad here, and my body was becoming so weak because I couldn't get the nutrients I needed. I was doing laundry by hand one day and was literally so weak that I couldn't wring all my clothes out very well. I didn't realize how tired I could get so quick. And that was hard for me, because I had always been physically strong.

I thought about how I couldn't even drive anywhere for months because I didn't have a Sudanese license yet. I couldn't just go somewhere after work because it would be dark. I couldn't just grab something at the local supermarket because the market was too far to walk to in order to get something quick.

I thought about how I was tired of fighting the gnats and flies every single day. They were always around, always annoying, and I got frustrated with them when I was trying to work on my computer or read a book. There were large ants, and they were always in our sugar and it would have been nice sometimes to put my spoon in and not have to shake any ants off. They also crawled right onto your foot if you stood in one place for even a second. One morning it was dark, and I stood still to try and push the kitchen door open and I had ants on me that fast. Another time I went to put my running shoes on and my toe touched something. I looked, and there was a big frog in my shoe.

Every morning, just making coffee was this huge ordeal. I had to carry all my coffee stuff with me, walk to the dining room where our key was kept, walk to the kitchen, not forgetting to carry two cups of filtered water with me along with my armful of stuff, set all my stuff down to unlock the kitchen, look for matches, light the gas stove and set the water to boiling, go brush my teeth, go back to make the coffee, carry all my stuff back to the dining room to put the key back, and finally go back to my room to have a nice cup of coffee during my quiet time with God. This was all while also carrying a flashlight. It took almost half an hour to do all this just for one cup of coffee. I missed just touching the button and having my coffee start and it not being instant coffee.

I missed turning on a light at 5:30 a.m. and reading my Bible. I had to light a kerosene lantern, which is a yellow flame that doesn't give much light, just to sit and read my Bible before work. The city cut the power every night at midnight, and it was off till 7:00 a.m.

I missed just getting in my shower and all my stuff would already be there. Here I had to drag all my stuff to the shower, because it is a community shower, and we all shared, so we don't leave our stuff to clutter up the place. More than once I forgot my towel and had to dry off with my T-shirt.

Every single night there were lots of dogs that howled and growled and fought, and all throughout the night, there were drums beating somewhere at any given time, and there was a club playing loud music all night until 7:00 a.m., because that is when they closed. I missed waking in the night to silence or even to the hum of an air conditioning unit.

I missed huge department stores that had everything you needed. An exciting day for me was when we heard that a container had come in because we knew that there would be a new selection of used clothes in the market to pick from. I couldn't go get hairspray or perfume or toothpaste or eyeliner or nail polish remover whenever I ran out. There was none. I missed ice cream and ice and gummy bears. Boy, did I miss gummy bears!

I missed going for a run with my headphones. I couldn't wear them because traffic doesn't watch out for me; I had to watch out for it. And people always wanted me to stop and talk, and it was very hard not to be irritated because I just wanted to run! I had to respond because Jesus would and so I stopped and talked.

I really missed putting my clothes in a washer and dryer. I got so tired of hauling water and doing each piece of laundry by hand. It was hard work, especially sheets.

What if I went back home and was just "normal" like most of the western world and had my normal job, in a normal country, living a normal life? Was I doing what I was created to do? I could never let my mind dwell on the "what ifs" because if I did, I would quit. I couldn't let myself think too long about home, because it hurt when I did. I couldn't think too long about the food I missed or malls or washing machines and dryers or even being able to buy a bottle of hair spray!

Little did I know that just a few months later I would be moving to a place much, much harsher than this. These things that I complained about later looked like heaven to me. Even as I write this book, I laugh now because I actually love my life in Sudan now, just the way it is. I became a part of the culture. Even my Sudanese friends now call me Sudanese woman! Simplicity looks great to me now. Giving up stuff to gain peace and joy is a journey. There is no easy road that leads to it. It is a continuous journey and the ever present speed bump raises up when you least expect it.

The statistics show that most missionaries quit in the first year, over 80 percent, because it is hard, and sometimes we feel like quitting. That is when I had to focus not on *why* I was doing a thing but on *Who* I was doing a thing for. Missions had to be about going after my desire, and my desire had to be Jesus Christ. He had to be the only reason I did a thing. He had to be what consumed me. If my desire ever changed, and if I let anything else consume me, I would quit. Only Jesus could inspire me to overcome. He had to remain my desire.

I found myself amazed sometimes that I once worked for a Christian ministry in a third world country and saw little physical evidence of spiritual life there sometimes. On the surface, it seemed to be more about the business of ministry and meeting timelines and quotas and financial obligations. I was naïve about ministry. I thought that people would be excited to break out of the walls of their daily habitation and go minister to the people.

I was really surprised to see that where I was, the work was their ministry and they mostly stayed within the confines of our small compound only engaging each other or other NGOs in community life. I had gained a real understanding of the scripture where David encouraged himself in the Lord. There were very few there to encourage me in the Lord spiritually after working hours. I learned about total dependence on God. This is what they told us about in Missions School. This is what we were told we would encounter many times in the mission field. People would do the works, but the intimacy with God would be gone if they wrapped themselves up in the works and lost their desire for intimacy, if they were there for any other reason than His heart alone.

I am learning that it is by the grace of God and walking with Him on this narrow road of love that I don't grow cold. Sometimes you find yourself having to deal with a culture that is so skewed in their thinking that if you don't stay on this road with God, you can become frustrated and cynical toward the people you are ministering to or working alongside. This is not just in Africa, it is in every nation of the world. Everywhere, there are people who are skewed in their thinking but we still have to love them. If I didn't stay close to the burnings of His heart and stay on the narrow road with Him, it would be very easy to become frustrated and hurt by the culture of a people and by the ways of a people and not necessarily individuals.

Corruption is a very real part of the culture in third world countries that I have visited. It wasn't something that was rampant among the general population but if a person had some sort of power, either in the marketplace or the city or state government, you could almost always bet on running into corruption at some point. How then could a person love a people with a mindset such as this? It could be difficult at times, because if one was not careful, you could look at everyone with suspicion and trust no one. How, then, could I continue to love the people with the love of God?

That was the key. You had to love with the love of God. When you were looking at people through His eyes and seeing with His heart, you really could love like Him, even your enemy. I always wondered how it could be possible, but I have learned the truth of this living in Africa. I have truly felt compassion for those who had wronged me, and I remained loyal to loving them and I treated them the same as I always had, with love and kindness. I could only do this from the abiding place of God. When we abide in His love and understand our position with Him as a son, nothing can separate us from this love. This is the love that we love others with.

Being in the mission field I was so excited because I thought I would be working and living with those who were of like mind and like faith, all having the same goal, and all going in the same direction spiritually. It didn't take long for me to learn that no matter how much we would like it to be so, it is not. Although we were of like mind concerning the work at hand, our spirits were sometimes not like-minded. It is very hard to stay in the corporate mind-set when it comes to your relationship with Jesus, especially when everyone has his own way of knowing Him. In the west, we go to church and conferences and revival meetings, and everyone gets fired up and excited about the presence of God, and we go where we can find like-minded people. We leave these meetings with a renewed vigor and hunger for the things of the kingdom of God and even new friendships with people *just like us.*

I found that what I learned in Missions 101 in Mozambique rang truer every day. There were no conferences in the mission field, at least not in a language you could understand. There were no churches that worshipped the way you are used to. Many times, there weren't people to pray with, because I couldn't speak their language yet. Even my fellow missionaries sometimes came from different faiths, depending upon the ministry I was with at the time, so I found myself bobbing on this spiritual ocean looking for the ship I came in on to come and rescue me. It is vital and necessary to encourage yourself in the Lord. If you don't encourage yourself and keep yourself afloat and stirred up, you die. You simply die spiritually,

No matter where others were spiritually, whether they were flying high with Holy Spirit or walking way behind or ahead of Him, I had to maintain my personal walk with the Lord and I kept my focus on why I was on the mission field, Jesus and only Jesus. A personal relationship with Him is paramount for a fruitful, healthy, loving walk with Jesus. Relying on corporate words or worship, or your love for the ministry, or even spiritual fellowship cannot sustain a person in any situation much less the third world mission field. I knew that my walk with the Lord had to be just that, my walk. It had to be sustainable.

One night my finger started hurting for no reason and swelling. The next day I began to experience solid and constant pain in my finger. As the day progressed, the pain and swelling got worse. Puss started to form, and this blood and puss balloon formed on my finger. The local Sudanese ladies were telling me that it was a parasite from the river water, which is what we wash our laundry in, which is also where people bathed, defecated, and urinated, and animals doing the same.

This parasite took up residence in my finger, and the ladies were saying that they had either lost their nail or remained with a permanently disfigured finger because of this same parasite attacking them. One lady had to go for surgery, another's bone showed through, all these horror stories!

I was also told by the ladies, all having experienced this parasite, that it would be a minimum of seven days before the pain even subsided. And all the while, the parasite would continue to eat. I said *no*! I called on my prayer team in the USA, via email of course. Then I took communion twice a day, even at 3:00 a.m., because I was in so much pain I couldn't even sleep, seriously. I took communion believing in His Blood poured out for me and

I believed in and counted on my personal and intimate relationship with Him. I also started on antibiotics. I was crying and hadn't slept in two nights. All I could do was call upon the name of Jesus and His Blood! All I could do was call upon Him to save me! He came. In just thirty-six hours my pain was completely gone! I had had only one antibiotic tablet, so it could not have been that already. The ladies came from all over our compound to see. I was tapping my finger against my desk. I was slapping it to show them I had no pain! Just two hours before, I was in excruciating pain and suddenly, it was gone!

They were saying, "It can only be a miracle! This cannot be! Look at my scar, I know!!" they said. All day I told them how Jesus came in the midst of my pain, because I was like the persistent widow crying out until He came (Luke 18:1-8). I had no other to save me. He was my only hope. The doctor stuck a needle in it, and nothing would come out, so even he could do nothing. In fact, it hurt worse. I cried and I called and I hoped and I never quit calling. I fell asleep with His name on my lips. I awoke with His name on my lips. He came! He came! I thought about the Israelites in the desert, "I can't do this. It's just too hard. I want to go back to Egypt where I at least had lentils!" And my spirit kept crying out, "You cannot quit! You just call upon the name of the Lord and believe, and He *will come!*" He did.

A few days after the finger incident, I thought that everyone had left after work as we had half days on Saturdays. As I was washing my clothes with my good hand, letting the skin on my other hand heal, a local lady, who was always the last to leave, because she cooked lunch for the workers, stopped to help me do my laundry. I tried to tell her no, because she worked so hard as it was and still had to go home to her own family and fix dinner and such. She couldn't speak good English, but I knew she understood me but she wouldn't be stopped. She washed all my clothes as I rinsed them. We worked side-by-side in silence, and I was so amazed that she would even wash my personal items.

In Sudan, underwear were so very personal and no one washes anyone else's underwear! Talk about laying your pride down! God was showing me so much about losing my pride that week and coming to Him as a little child and allowing others to help me. He was also showing me how much these people loved me. I was becoming one of them as I loved them and learned from them, even through the trials and struggles of everyday life.

The dry season in Sudan arrived with dust storms and heat so extreme that I actually fried an egg on a rock. Almost every night it was above one hundred degrees all throughout the night. We tossed, and we turned in our puddles of sweat and waited for the morning to come. Sometimes, in my frustration, I laid there and wondered to myself how I could continue to survive in this place where it never gets cool. I couldn't even read for too long before bed, because even my headlamp caused more heat. We all slept fitfully only to wait on the coming dawn. And yet, when I awoke, tired as I was, I found myself in God's Word, still sweating, yet gaining new strength for each day. Another man that I worked with said the same thing. We couldn't think about next week or even the next night, only each day as it came. God gives us enough mercy and grace for each day. They really are *new* every single morning. It is up to us to partake of them. Reminds me of gathering fresh manna in the wilderness. Hmmm.....

During the dry summers, the days remained in the 120s. Each night I moved my bed outside my tent and was treated to the most beautiful starry sky. I fell asleep staring at the heavens and thanking God for His love for us. I fell asleep thinking about Jacob and him saying, "Surely the lord is in this place." I had such great sleep, even in the 100 degree nights! This remained my permanent sleeping place, outside under the blanket of heaven looking at the Southern Cross constellation, my favorite one, falling asleep in wonder at His creation, knowing He watched over me as I slept, and also feeling a lot cooler outside my tent. I did sleep enclosed in a bug hut that sat on my bed.

When we drove to town every day, there was so much dust and dirt that my hair had a white coating by the time I returned. Each morning I made the one hour trek at 6:30 a.m. to our nearest city to get to the meat market early enough to buy our meat. In Akuem, I pretty much gave up early morning coffee, because in order to have any, I would have had to make a fire and then wait for the water to boil. All that took an hour extra, so I would just mix up some Tang and off I went. The journey most of the way was over bumpy dirt roads, across fields, tilting precariously to one side as I went down into ravines off of the main dirt road. Every morning I drove past the cattle camps where they *smoke* the cows. It makes me laugh when I say that. The cattle herders burn cow chips, which smolder and surround the cows with smoke to ward off mosquitoes and sickness in their cows. The cattle are very peaceful and seem to enjoy it. Pretty crazy. This is also what the people burn in their huts to ward off mosquitoes.

While in town, I could not walk ten feet without people of every single age, male and female, asking me for money. It never let up, and they were very persistent about it. I got to know the vendors that I went to each time, so they didn't make me go through the whole price haggling bit anymore.

The flies were so incredibly horrible in the northern part of South Sudan. They never left you alone. When visiting the latrine after dark with flashlights, we had to hang them up high, because there were so many fat belligerent flies attacking our lights and faces if we didn't remove the headlamps from our heads. When I was ready to leave the latrine I grabbed my light and shook it like crazy as I literally ran out. And if you squatted too long, well never mind… I can really understand how the devil is connected to flies and the whole Beelzebub deal. They are annoying pests that never let up. That's how Satan is, he never lets up, so we have to find new ways to rid ourselves of his pestering. Hmm… shaking the Light at him? Works for the flies.

Ministry in a third world country tries and tests our patience when it comes to the needy, whether genuine or not. The people want whatever we have, and they don't hesitate to ask. It wears a person down sometimes. Even as I tried to find some peace and quiet in my tent, all of a sudden I would hear, "Kalowina, you give ball or balloon or sweets..." My tent was right next to the back fence, about ten yards from it, and the children would constantly call out to me. Every day they waited until I went to get my shower bucket and clothes in the evening, and there they were yelling through the fence. They would stand at that fence for half an hour constantly asking, even if I remained quiet and didn't say a word, or if I was engaged in a conversation with someone else.

One day I just started singing to them through my tent that I had no ball, only love to give away. They just laughed at that and enjoyed it. After that day, they would come to hear me sing! God has a great sense of humor.

Also there was no place that I could go to be alone. There was a path that ran along the outside of the fence near my tent, and I used to wonder if people stopped to stare at me while I read by flashlight at night or something, because I would hear them walking by and then it would get quiet. After living there for some time I quit worrying about those things because I was becoming used to life in Sudan. It just became a part of who I was and where I lived. I was learning how to live inside my invisible bubble and shut the outside world out even in the midst of it when I needed to. Some days though, it was most difficult and frustrating.

I looked at people like Heidi Baker, who has lines of people every Sunday right after church, and throughout the week, and she stops and listens to them, even saying no in love, but she listens. I had two adults one week ask me for money to put them through school, and I told them that I couldn't get money because there are no banks in Sudan to get American money from. Still they asked. I told them that I gave what I had to the children, still they asked. I even had people asking me to bring them computers from America next time I went. It just didn't register that we were not able to do this for them.

They saw my computer, my iPod, the place where I worked and lived with nice brick buildings, and they saw it as having a lot of money, even if the buildings were not mine. I couldn't make them understand otherwise, no matter what I said. This made it so hard to even give little things sometimes because it just added fuel to the fire that you had stuff. I found myself learning even more about patience than ever before, because I knew that all of their requests were valid and genuine. All I could do was pray with them that God be their answer in all things and help whenever I could. And I learned how to say no in a non-offensive, non-abrasive way. I learned the extremes of diplomacy, compassion, patience, and perseverance in all of it, not growing weary of listening and caring. It is a daily journey of walking it out in each situation. We never stop learning or growing in these things, therefore we need to enjoy the journey.

I was also gaining a deeper understanding of the scripture in Isaiah 43:18, "Forget the former things; do not dwell on the past. See, I am doing a new thing! Now it springs up; do you not perceive it? I am making a way in the desert and streams in the wasteland."

As I looked back on my former life of comfort and ease in the USA compared to Sudan, I didn't dwell on my past life of comfort. I rarely went there to the place of physical comfort, because I had found a new place of comfort and security in the desert, in the wasteland of Sudan. God always wants to do a new thing. He wants us to "See it and perceive it." He always makes a way for me to walk on the path of grace through this dry and weary land. In the morning when I woke up, I felt the wellness of my soul. I felt the peace that surpassed all understanding in my natural mind. I have never slept better at any time in my life than I did and still do in Sudan. Even now, when I come for visits to the

USA, I never sleep well. My mind and body have grown accustomed to the place where I belonged, where God had called me to, the Sudan.

It was truly well with my soul, even though my body screamed sometimes. I slept outside at night with only a thin layer of net between myself and the world. I slept like a baby with a belly full of milk. It was only my complete faith in my God that allowed me to do this. In the USA, I would lock all the doors and have an alarm set in my house before I could sleep comfortably. My, what a change the Lord had done in me.

I remember the first rains of the season when I was in the driest part of South Sudan, in Akuem. I never believed that I would ever see grass in that place, even though the locals were telling me that it would be. With that first rain, out of the dessert, grass came forth. Our entire compound was dirt, pure dirt, not a shred of grass, even dead grass, anywhere. Where on earth does the grass spring up from then? After the grass came forth, I bent down and just ran my hand across the top of a patch. It was sheer joy, and I actually smiled because it felt so good to touch grass again for the first time since being in Akuem. I would never take grass for granted again. Even as I am editing this book on a short break in the USA, it is summertime and I find myself walking outside to walk barefoot in the grass and still I am smiling.

This new grass in Sudan from a seemingly dead place caused me to think about the dreams and thoughts of our hearts and what we have given up on because we thought, "How could there be anything to grow from here? It surely must be a dead place." I thought about how many people had given up on the dreams of their hearts. They have told themselves that it must surely be a dead thing, because they see no life there anymore. I looked at all this dirt that I was daily surrounded by. I remembered worshiping near my tent those many weeks ago and how excited I was when I saw just one tiny sprig of green standing there alone, a fragile shoot surrounded by the dry and parched earth. I looked at that tiny thing, and I said, "Surely there is hope in the desert."

God looks at our fragile dreams and thoughts, and He sees them sometimes standing alone there, standing against the winds and storms of life, when all else seems dead. And even when we lay them down thinking they were not really what was to be for us. And we bury them there in the desert of lost dreams and walk away, thinking they are forever gone, because there is nothing to water them with, no one to care for them. And then the rains come; and then life comes. And out of a seemingly dead place, life comes in abundance. It shoots up and spreads across the desert and overtakes that dead place with new life.

> Behold, I am doing a new thing! Now it springs forth; do you not perceive it and know it and will you not give heed to it? I will even make a way in the wilderness and rivers in the desert.
>
> Isaiah 43:19

The Lord was showing me with that single little shoot standing alone of the things yet to come. He shows us little things, and He spurs our hearts to wonder, gently asking us, "Do you not perceive what I am starting just for you? Do you not know it by this small thing I am showing you? Will you not give heed to it My beloved?"

I learned in those harsh living conditions that I could either experience the harshness of living there, or I could experience the even better grace of God. Complaining never changes anything, it just heaps more stress on the situation. So, if I look at all my life situations through the eyes and heart of Jesus, I can see His hand in everything, and find His grace to endure and even overcome and enjoy all things.

I used to get upset when I saw scorpions in my tent. Soon I just stepped on them without a second thought, and I got on with whatever I was about. I used to get upset because I had nowhere to be alone and enjoy reading my Bible. My tent might have scorpions, so I couldn't relax in there. There was always noise and people in the office. There were always people around the compound and at night it was too dark to see, and if I used my headlamp I got a nose full of gnats.

So, I got up early before anyone, took all my books and pen and computer music (my iPod broke), and found the tallest truck on our compound and climbed in. There was my quiet place with Jesus. And when all the tall trucks were gone, I set my chair in between two small ones, set my coffee cup on the running board, my computer on another chair, and there you had it, my quiet place. There was always an answer if I looked at the world through God's eyes. He always makes a way. I want to encourage people to look for God in everything, to look for His way. It makes living in your world so much easier, regardless of where that is. Never grow weary, just keep moving forward.

I know that there are so many missionaries around the world who are in much tougher places than I. There are people all over the world who are not missionaries who are in tougher places than I. So I don't complain, I really don't. I have learned to be content no matter what. Every new place I go, it gets a little harder. If I am called to Sudan, then I can't come from the beach resort straight to the Sahara. There has to be transition. God had to take me *through* places to get me ready for the *to* places. The next place should require more than the last. That is transition. With the measure that I use what He has equipped me with, the more of His grace He pours out on me. I heard Him calling then, and even now, "Come, let's do this together for My grace will take us through." Our journey with Jesus is all about transition, transformation and fullness of life. Where there is life, something had to die, a seed sown. The hard places in ministry are usually what bring us to a place of walking closer to the Lord. If I want to look like Jesus, I must welcome transition and transformation. I used to wonder how the disciples immediately left everything to follow Jesus. They didn't ask Him where they were going or what they were going to do. They just went. I believe that they saw His love. They saw that He would stop for them, the ones placed in front of Him that day. Jesus showed them how much easier it was to follow than to be in control. He showed them how much easier it was to stop and love one than it was to stop for the masses and have big conferences. It was all that He asked them to do, to follow Him. He was always there, and where He was, there was peace.

> "Come, follow Me," Jesus said, "and I will make you fishers of men." At once they left their nets and followed Him.
>
> Mathew 4:19-20

about the author

Carolyn Figlioli is actively pursuing the footsteps of the Lord in South Sudan, where she has lived for almost three years. She currently resides at the Iris Yei Children's Village in Yei, Sudan, where she ministers to the youth. She also teams up with other missionaries and local pastors to reach out to the local Sudanese church body by speaking and ministering at churches, local conferences, hospitals, and prisons.

Carolyn is currently pioneering an Iris Sudan base in Aweil, where she ministers to the street boys of Aweil. She also visits the poor and displaced people in the Internationally Displaced People camps in Aweil, where refugees have come from as far north as Khartoum and Darfur to live, away from the violence of the north.

She loves the poor and the orphan and the widow. Her heart is to see street children reunited with their families and to build a community where orphans and widows can make a home together, living and loving as small family units, in their own homes.

Carolyn travels twice a year to the USA and is available to speak at churches, conferences, community gatherings, and other places where people want to hear about what the Lord is doing on the earth and how they can partner with Him and find joy in it, no matter the calling.

You may contact Carolyn with comments or questions at www.called2follow.com.